Cool Party, Mom!
THE OTHER THREE WORDS EVERY MOTHER LOVES TO HEAR

MARNIE ANN PACINO

Cover and interior art also by:
Marnie Ann Pacino

© 2010 Marnie Ann Pacino. All rights reserved

ISBN 1453766634
EAN 9781453766637

Printed in the United States of America

www.coolpartymom.com

This book is also available in several electronic formats.

For Andrew, Nicholas, Gabriela
Jessica and Ben

**A special thanks
to my husband, mom, and friends
for encouraging, persuading, and badgering me
to sit down and write!**

**....and a whole bucket of gratitude
to my friend, P.J. Jobst, for saving me
from drowning in typos!**

COOL CONTENTS

INTRODUCTION	1
THE ELEVEN COMMANDMENTS OF KID PARTIES	3
THE COMPLETE GUIDE TO A WILD WEST PARTY	15
THE COMPLETE GUIDE TO A GROSS PARTY	35
THE COMPLETE GUIDE TO AN UNDER THE SEA PARTY	51
THE COMPLETE GUIDE TO A CAMPOUT	67
THE COMPLETE GUIDE TO A FIESTA	89
THE COMPLETE GUIDE TO A MAD SCIENCE PARTY	105
THE COMPLETE GUIDE TO A COOL LUAU	125
THE COMPLETE GUIDE TO A PRINCESS PARTY	143
THE COMPLETE GUIDE TO A JUNGLE SAFARI	157
THE COMPLETE GUIDE TO AN OUTER SPACE PARTY	173
THE COMPLETE GUIDE TO A PIRATE PARTY	191
THE COMPLETE GUIDE TO A SLUMBER PARTY	205
THE COMPLETE GUIDE TO A SCAVENGER HUNT	231
RANDOM TIPS	237
EASY PEASY INDEX	239

INTRODUCTION

Birthdays are more than mere milestones in a child's journey. For a mother, they are a rare opportunity to create a lasting memory for her child- a moment that child will carry for the rest of their life. **No pressure there.**

Even with one child, you're still looking at a dozen themes, a dozen menus, and dozens of party activities to plan over the course of a lightning-fast childhood. If you're anything like me, every single year, you will feel compelled to spend an insane amount of time thinking about and planning for, this assessment of your mothering skills.

Over the last 20 years, I've hosted countless parties for the awesome kids in my life. I've learned many lessons along the way. At the urging of my friends and family, I gathered my ideas, picked the brains of fellow moms, and put all of the best stuff in one fun, sensible, easy-to-follow, foolproof, no-nonsense, instructional guide!

We're talking *classic* kid parties, with real ideas that stand the test of time. You won't find parties-in-a-box or trendy themes here. However, each guide is designed to work for almost any similar theme. So, if your little guy is just begging for a party that revolves around that famous sea sponge, you will find plenty of help in the Under the Sea Party Guide.

Now, if you bought this book (or it was a gift from, clearly, the smartest person you know), I'm going to assume: (A) you don't have a personal party planner on staff, and (B) you are perfectly capable of holding a pair of scissors correctly.

On the following pages, you will find everything else you need, to plan your way to the *other* three words every mother loves to hear… "Cool party, Mom!"

2

CHAPTER 1

THE ELEVEN COMMANDMENTS OF KID PARTIES

Over the years, I've compiled a set of common sense, party-planning rules for myself. They keep me organized, on task, on budget, and well within the boundaries of sanity and social acceptability (most of the time).

#1 THE GUEST LIST!

So, you've decided to plan a party. **How many little monsters can you *really* handle at one time?** For kids under the age of five, I have two imperatives:

1. **The number of guests equals the Birthday Kid's age.** (A four-year-old invites four kids.)
2. **Under five, parents stay!** (See Commandment #11 for details.)

Once you enter the uber-sensitive world of politically correct stupidity (i.e. grade school), things get a bit stickier. Most schools have an unspoken rule regarding birthday parties: "If you invite one, you should invite them all." This leaves you with three, equally unappetizing choices:

- Invite everyone and make yourself crazy.
- Throw a covert party and swear all the kids to secrecy.
- Limit the guest list and prepare to receive a few nasty looks in the carpool lane.

Most of you, like me, will opt for the third choice. The new challenge becomes finding a way to invite a chosen few, without stepping on Bobby Stinkypants (or his mother's) self-esteem. Believe me; I completely understand why you don't want to invite him. There is *always* that one nightmare kid who picks fights, whines, complains, and generally requires way too much attention. Not so surprisingly, I've found that the apple does not fall far from the tree with this sort of kid.

My advice is to forgo passing out that stack of brightly colored envelopes in class. Instead, **opt to hand-deliver your invitations.** Most of the children probably live nearby, and will be intrigued by the personal touch. Better yet, Bobby Stinkypants and his mother will be none-the-wiser.

If perchance, Momma Stinkypants confronts you (it happens): be polite, don't over-explain yourself, and do what all the smart moms do- **blame your husband.** "Oh sorry, hubby has me on a very tight budget, maybe next year." Give her a "what-can-ya-do" smile, and make a hasty exit. This does not make you a coward. Remember: it's your money, it's your time, and it's your energy. Again, you don't want that lasting memory to include a Bobby Stinkypants meltdown!

"Okay, I get all of that, but really, how many should I invite?" Once kids are in school, unless you have an army of adults to help, I suggest sticking to the **age-equals-number-of-guests-formula** with one very important caveat; Including the Birthday Kid, the **final count should always be an even number**. (A ten-year-old gets to invite nine guests.) Call me a cynic, but I am convinced that from the first day of Kindergarten, children become experts in playground politics, long before they master their ABCs. Even without Bobby Stinkypants, catty little cliques are not uncommon among six-year-olds. **An even number will give everyone an ally.** This is especially important to keep in mind when you're planning a sleepover. Don't be fooled; pre-teen girls can be incredibly vicious!

#2 THE INVITES!

So you've conquered the dilemma of how many to invite. Now it's time to figure out how to get them to come. I've always been disappointed in the selection of pre-printed invites available; the good ones are usually expensive, and the cheap ones tend to be poorly designed. So, unless you find something simply irresistible, **skip the pre-packaged invitations.**

Instead, put on your thinking cap, and find a way to create that enticing first impression. Homemade invitations or simple Invite Favors with Invite Tags (more on these later) will do the trick. Don't panic. Making invitations is much easier than it sounds. You do not have to be a scrapbook diva with a dedicated craft room and a glue stick tucked behind your ear. If you have a computer and a printer, you are well on your way!

Head to your local office supply store. There will be dozens of paper designs to match your chosen party theme. If you're having a Wild West Party, try tan paper that looks like parchment. If you're having a Space Party, choose paper with moons and stars. Once you get home, close the door to your home office, open your word processing software, and start typing!

"What should the invite say?" Well of course, you'll need to add the standard ***Who, What, When and Where***, but then use a little imagination and add a simple rhyme or short funny poem. If you don't have a knack for rhyming, I've added wording examples to each *Complete Guide* to get you started. If you still have trouble, online rhyming dictionaries can be a huge help.

- If you're having a Sleepover, be sure to include a list of things to bring like sleeping bags, pajamas, and flashlights.
- If you're having a Gross Party, remind your guests to dress appropriately.

INVITE FAVORS & TAGS

I've found that passing out small, theme-related **Invite Favors**, is an easy, inexpensive way to get kids excited about a party. **Start with a trip to your local dollar store.** If you're planning a Safari Party, grab a herd of small, beanbag animals. Pick up a bucket of plastic sandbox shovels for a Luau or a handful of Magic Wands for a Princess Party. On the following pages, you will find tons of fun, inexpensive Invite Favor ideas.

When you get home, create a smaller version of a traditional invitation, and attach it to each Invite Favor. **Invite Tags** are super simple to make, even with minimal computer skill:

1. Using your word processing software, create a new Document.
2. Insert a Table, two columns wide and four rows high.
3. Type your invite information in the first box.
4. Copy and Paste the information into the remaining seven boxes.
5. Print the Invite Tags on your cool theme-related paper.
6. Cut them apart.
7. Use a hole-punch, and ribbon or string to attach them to your Invite Favors.

"But, I really, really can't find my way out of a paper bag when it comes to computers!" No problem. Just cut your theme-related paper into four, six, or eight equal pieces. Use colorful markers to hand-write your party information, and don't forget to let the Birthday Kid help!

Whether you are passing out homemade invitations or Invite Favors, they should be **delivered four to six weeks before the party**. Follow up with a phone **call, a week before the party**, to get a final confirmed guest count.

COOL IDEAS FOR INVITES!
- Use cardstock to prevent the string from tearing through the punched holes.
- Fancy-up the Invite Tags by cutting them apart with zigzag scissors.
- If you don't have enough room for everything, use both sides.

#3 FORMULATE A PLAN!

The invites are out. There's no turning back. In a matter of weeks, you will have a house full of kids staring at you and waiting to be entertained. Make it easy on yourself by creating an outline of your Party Schedule.

For a two-hour party, use the **3-2-1 Method**:
- **Three** things to do - games, activities, or crafts
- **Two** times to eat - snacks and cake
- **One** finale - opening presents or pulverizing a piñata

This will help you keep your sanity and keep the party moving. Most activities should last about 20 minutes (the approximate attention span of any 5-15 year old). **Stay flexible and keep a few ideas on reserve** in case the kids get bored. If you are planning a Sleepover, you will obviously need more things to do, so be sure to choose a combination of high-energy activities like physical games, running, or swimming, and low energy activities like crafts, cooking, or movies.

COOL TIP!
When parent attendance is mandatory (sometimes even when it's not), **always assume that at least one parent will show up with extra kids in tow**. Yes, it's annoying. Yes, it's rude. **Avoid being frazzled and prepare for it.** Buy a few more party favors. Let the extra kids join in on the fun, or set aside a separate place with coloring books, blocks, or movies to entertain the little party crashers.

#4 GET ORGANIZED!

Lists, glorious lists! Planning a kid's party can be overwhelming. So, grab a spiral notebook and keep yourself organized with a few key lists:

- Things to Buy or Order
- Things to Do a Week Before
- Things to Do the Day Before
- Things to Do Party Day
- Things Other People Can Do

That last one is the most important. Don't hesitate to delegate tasks to your family and close friends. Have your husband lug the folding chairs or ask your best friend to pick up the balloons. One of the requirements of being a *Cool* Party Mom is remaining cool. The best way to do this is to **ask for help when you need it!**

COOLEST TIP OF ALL!
Find a teenage helper (babysitter, neighbor, or niece) to assist. Most teen girls love craft projects, helping with little kids, and organizing. If there's resistance, offer cash!

#5 HUNT AND GATHER!

Much like pre-printed invitations, themed paper goods are often expensive. With a little thrifty imagination, you can still plan "The-Best-Princess-Party-Ever-For-All-Eternity" without surrendering to matchy-matchy paper products, and more importantly, without breaking the bank.

After your Party Schedule and Lists are made, head back to the dollar store. You will find plenty of plates, napkins, favors, decorations and craft project materials. If you can't find what you need there, check the Internet. You can save big bucks, even with shipping costs, by shopping at sites that sell by the dozen or in bulk. (Keep in mind, if you are ordering supplies online, you should start shopping a month before the party to allow time for shipping, returns, and exchanges.)

Next stop: your local supercenter. This is where I pick up inexpensive items like serving platters and snack-size Crock-Pots. (These are perfect for serving cocktail weenies, cheese dips, and melted chocolate - a solid investment for less than ten dollars.) After you leave the Housewares Department, head over to the Pet Department. Yes, I said the Pet Department! About 15 years ago, I picked up several one-gallon, glass fishbowls at the supercenter. I fill them with punch; use them to serve dry snacks; load them with candy; and have even found ways to use them for games and activities. They're cheap, sturdy, and easy to clean.

Finally, stop by your local fabric or craft store. Dig through the clearance racks to find discount craft supplies, tablecloths, and accent fabrics. Most of the time, you will find exactly what you need without stepping foot inside a party store!

COOL TIP!
While you're shopping, consider stocking your party arsenal with things like: three-tier servers, fondue pots, and punch bowls. Odds are this isn't the last party you'll host. Better yet, try to convince your best friend to split the cost (and storage) of these items. What are the chances you'll both need them at the same time?

#6 CLEAN!

If you don't have the luxury of having a live-in maid, pick a room, any room: living room, garage, basement, or backyard. Two weeks before the party, **pick a room and clear out the clutter.** When the kids walk in, you want them transported to another world, not tripping over your entire collection of home improvement magazines! Get rid of it! Remove collectibles, tame electrical cords, and put away your cherished pictures of Grandma. Even if your own kids know not to touch certain things, that doesn't mean other people's children will, and nothing will bring a party to a screeching halt more than the sound of shattering glass. Once the Party Room is cleaned up and kid-friendly, **find a corner, and start stacking your supplies, decorations, chairs, party favors, etc.**

#7 DECORATE!

Timing is everything! If you are making or painting decorations or props for the party, do it the weekend before. This will help to avoid last minute catastrophes. Then, if possible, **start setting scene in the Party Room a few days ahead.** This will allow you to concentrate on organizing activities and preparing the party food in the final hours.

When decorating, **focus your energy on the Party Room and the kitchen**. You can add a few touches to the front porch and the bathroom, but **leave the rest of the house as it is.** It's a kid's Party, not a house tour, and you don't want your little guests straying off into various parts of the house just because something pink and glittery caught their eye!

#8 COOK!

Kids are picky eaters; but generally, do not possess sophisticated taste buds. So, save your favorite Basil Bruschetta recipe for another time and **keep your menu simple and easy**.

For a two-hour kid's party, set out a fishbowl snack buffet with trail mix, grapes, gummy candies, etc. If the party is longer, add a small meal of rollups, pasta, etc. If you're planning a sleepover, add a late-night snack and breakfast. Also, keep in mind when you're dealing with kids, you might have to address some food allergies.

#9 TAKE LOTS OF PHOTOS!

Obviously, you're going to want lots of pictures from the big day, but even with copious pre-arranging and organizing, you will still have your hands full during the actual party. **This is a perfect task to delegate to your husband, friend, or teenage helper.** Remind them to take plenty of action shots of each guest. After the party, print them and include them with your Thank You Notes. (Even if it's just via email, you should still send Thank You Notes!)

COOL IDEA! After the Party, if you are somewhat tech-savvy, **organize your digital shots with movie-making software to create a slideshow**. This is actually a lot easier than it sounds. Try Microsoft Movie Maker that comes with most versions of Windows. Add your photos, videos, and music. Then burn the slideshow to CDs or email it to your guests. The whole process will take a few hours, but what a cool way to relax and appreciate your hard work. To top it off, you'll have an awesome keepsake for your own child. (Something you can pull out when he's a teenager telling you that *other people's* parents are much cooler!)

#10 OTHER PEOPLE'S KIDS!

Speaking of other people, dealing with other people's kids can be a challenge. Not all families share the same rules or discipline techniques. However, for eight hours a day in school, all children are programmed to behave. This begins and ends with two words: **order and activity**.

To keep things from getting out of hand, it's a good idea to **pretend you are a teacher for the day**. Make a plan, take charge, and speak up when you have something to say to the group, "Okay monkeys (campers, princesses, etc.) we're going to move on to the next fun activity. I need you to XYZ." This will maintain order with most kids from age 5-15.

If you find you have a child on the verge of a melt-down (oddly, this is often the Birthday Kid), ask them to help you with something in the other room. Walk them out of earshot, look them in the eye, and inquire about the problem. Listen and try to address their issue. If it is your own kid, more than likely, they are just excited and overwhelmed. Tell them to take a deep breath, and remind them that they don't want to miss the fun because they're in trouble. If someone is "being a meanie", wait a few minutes and make a general announcement of the party rules. If there doesn't seem to be a specific cause for the melt-down, make it clear that you need the behavior to stop and explain the consequences if it continues. Most of the time, this calm, direct, private request will make all the difference in the world! Whatever you do, do not lose your cool. It's a party. Remember: cherished memory!

#11 AGE MATTERS!

If you're a mom planning a party for your own child, please don't take offense to this section. I do not think you are completely inept and lacking a brain. I felt compelled to add it for the people who do not have experience caring for children on a daily basis (i.e. grandmas, aunts, newly adoptive parents, and dare I say, dads?)

When planning a kid's party, **it is most important to determine what is age-appropriate and what is not**. Little ones won't want to karaoke for hours, and pre-teens will have no interest in Deep Sea Animal Charades.

Here are some quick guidelines to help plan for the different stages of childhood:

TODDLERS
Kids younger than five generally don't have the capacity to appreciate an afternoon of organized activities and meticulously planned menus. So...

- Follow my advice, and **make parental attendance mandatory!** They can handle their own child's meal choices, potty breaks, and meltdowns.
- Keep the decorations simple with balloons, streamers, and colorful plates. (Little hands tend to gravitate towards the mouth. The last thing you want to do is spend the entire party preventing little Cowpokes from eating your decorative straw!)
- Instead of serving a sit-down meal, set out a few divided snack trays with diced fruits, raisins, crackers, cookies, and cereals.
- Make cupcakes in mini-muffin pans instead of baking an entire cake.
- Keep plenty of wet wipes, towels, and wash cloths within reach.
- Fill separate laundry baskets with toy cars, large building blocks, floor puzzles, noisy pot lids, and wooden spoons. (Don't put them all out at once!)
- Play games like Copy Cat, Animal Charades, and Beanbag Toss.
- Little ones require more maintenance and tire easily, so don't plan too much, and remember to stay flexible!

AGES 5 to 7

Once in school, kids are used to being managed *en masse*, and have the capacity to follow directions. Best of all, these kids are easily amused!

- Play traditional games like Hot Potato, Duck-Duck-Goose, and Musical Chairs.
- Plan a few simple craft projects, or fascinate them with a few science experiments.
- Most 5-7 year olds are not very adventurous when it comes to trying new foods, so prepare conventional party food like hot dogs, pizza, and chips.
- Kids are also still a bit clumsy at this age, so serve smaller portions on plates at the table, and use sports bottles or cups with lids for drinks.
- Sleepovers can be unpredictable with 1st and 2nd graders. Rely on the parents to determine if their own child can handle a night away. Be prepared to make a middle of the night phone call home to mom, and most importantly, try to plan activities so that any child who is not sleeping over won't miss too much of the fun.

AGES 8 to 12

This is when we generally separate the boys from the girls. Mixed-gender parties can still be fun, but interests tend to veer in opposite directions. Your menu can be more elaborate, craft activities can be more involved, and the games can be more competitive. Bottom line, it will take a bit more work to impress pre-teens, but this when you can let your *cool* party mom imagination run wild!

TEENS

Teen parties can be a challenge. Most of the ideas on the following pages are designed for younger children. However, all of the recipes can be used with great success for a teen party, and you might be surprised how a game of Duck-Duck-Goose will turn a group of stoic teens simply giddy!

- Unless the teen Birthday Kid requests it, don't go overboard with *theme-y* decorations. All teenagers really want is great food and space to socialize.
- Make sure you have music, movies, video games, and the Internet available (with usage guidelines, of course).
- Set up a volleyball net, karaoke machine, or plan a Neighborhood Scavenger Hunt.
- If it's a mixed-gender party, start the party with a clear announcement of the rules, and supervise at a responsible distance.

Those are the basics! On the following pages, I've organized parties by theme. Each theme has a *Complete Guide* to everything you'll need to plan a cool party. Don't try to do everything. Just pick a few, and **remember to have fun!**

CHAPTER 2

THE COMPLETE GUIDE TO A WILD WEST PARTY!

After a hard day on the range, all cowboys like to let loose and bust a rug. So, let's rustle up some grub, and have a rowdy good time at our old-fashioned shindig!

WILD WEST INVITES

REAL HORSESHOES

Call your local stable to find some real horseshoes; they don't have to be new. (If you live in the city, check online.) Clean the horseshoes with soap and water and let them dry on a stack of paper towels. Feed pieces of raffia or twine through the nail holes to attach Invite Tags. (See Chapter 1)

BADGES AND BANDANAS

Fold a red bandana into four squares and then diagonally into a triangle. Pin a metal or plastic sheriffs' badge in the middle to attach an Invite Tag. Several websites carry toy badges that you can personalize with each guest's name.

WANTED POSTERS

Print your Invites on tan parchment paper. Add a black and white photo of the Birthday Kid in the center of each. Roll up the Invites, and tie closed with pieces of raffia or twine.

Here's an example of how you might word your Wanted Poster Invites:

WANTED
A herd of mangy cowpokes to mosey on over
To Johnson Ranch for a ten-gallon celebration
In honor of Benjamin the Bandit's 10th Birthday!
September 23rd HIGH NOON
Dust off your boots and put on your fancy cowboy duds.
We'll have a dandy time makin' a ruckus and chowin' down on tasty vittles!
GIVE US A HOLLER! 555-5555
REWARD

WILD WEST FAVORS

Wild West favors are super easy to find. Check the dollar store and the Internet for things like: bandanas, harmonicas, deputy badges, water pistols, toy holsters, spurs, cowboy hats, toy jacks, marble sets, paddleballs, Chinese yo-yos, candy root beer barrels, licorice rope, chocolate coins, waxed paper taffy, old-fashioned rock candy on a stick, or golden-nugget bubblegum pouches.

FAVOR BAGS

Small, four or six inch, decorative tin pails are available at most local craft stores. These make great favor bags for a Wild West Party. You can also, fill them with crayons for an activity, or peanuts in the shell for table decorations.

SIX PACK FAVORS

Send each kid home with a six-pack of old-fashioned bottled root beer! They will love pretending to be cowpokes at the dinner table for the rest of the week!

MOO MIXER FAVORS

Battery-operated "Moo Mixers" have been around forever! These cow-print, kid-friendly, mini-blenders are a hit, even with adults. Add some milk, a squirt of chocolate syrup, and press the button-- instant chocolate milk! You can find them in most novelty stores and online for less than ten dollars each. They are worth every penny! (Don't forget to pick up an extra one for your man-child husband.)

WILD WEST DECORATIONS

BALES OF STRAW

Your local nursery should have plenty of inexpensive, straw bales to stack on your front porch. Add a length of coiled rope, a cowboy hat, and a pair of cowboy boots to complete the display. If you're brave, scatter a bit of straw around the Party Room floor and on the tables. After the party, have the Birthday Kid use a shop-vac to clean up the mess, and donate the leftover bales to a local animal shelter.

BANDANAS

What's a Wild West Party without bandanas? Tie them around the cowpokes as they arrive, or use them for crafts and games. You can also string a bunch of bandanas together (tying opposite corners), and hang them like triangle streamers in the Party Room. To find out how many you'll need to make streamers, figure the diagonal of the bandana, and subtract a few inches to tie a knot. A standard 22" bandana has a 31" diagonal. So, 20 tied together will make a streamer about 45 feet long.

WOODEN CRATES

Looks like the stagecoach just dropped off some supplies! Paint old cardboard boxes with a roller and a quart of brown latex paint from the hardware store. (Spray paint doesn't cover as well.) If your kids are old enough or you have a teenage helper, let them drag the boxes into the backyard and paint them for you; they don't have to be perfect. After the boxes dry completely, use a stencil and black craft paint to label the crates with words like *DYNAMITE or WHISKEY*. Stack the boxes in piles of two or three around the Party Room. Stuff some straw between the layers of boxes, and hang a coil of rope or a cowboy hat from the corner.

WOODEN SAWHORSES

Toss a few Mexican blankets over the top of a regular sawhorse. Add a cowboy hat or coil of rope to each end. These are great for blocking off restricted areas.

BURLAP BAGS

You can order burlap bags online, or pick up a few yards of burlap from the fabric store and make your own. Cut 2 ft x 3 ft pieces, and either sew or hot glue the seams together. Then, use a stencil and black craft paint to label each bag with words like *COFFEE, POTATOES, SUGAR, or FLOUR*. Once they dry, stuff the bags with crumpled newspaper and tie them closed with brown twine or raffia. Prop a few bags against a stack of *wooden* crates or on a bale of straw.

WANTED POSTERS

Use tan parchment paper to print Wanted Posters with black and white, grainy pictures of your outlaw guests. Give them a fun alias like *Dastardly Dave, Too Tall Tim, or Black Hat Bobby*. Add silly crimes like wearing stinky socks, stealing candy, riding horses backwards, snoring, or not cleaning their boots! Hang the fun posters around the Party Room.

WILD WEST STREET SIGN

- One 2x4 piece of wood
- Cardboard
- Black craft paint
- Paintbrush
- Staple gun
- Rope or zip-ties

Paint cardboard directional arrows that say things like *California 500 miles, Mexico 200 miles, and New York City 2,000 miles*. Staple the arrows to the front of the 2x4, and use rope or zip-ties to attach the signpost to your mailbox, porch column, or tree. Hop on the Web to figure out the real mileage from your house to the destination!

PAINTED SIGNS

Use black craft paint and cardboard to post Wild West saloon sayings like: *NO bandits!; NO shootin'; NO wrasslin'; NO spittin'; Vittles 5 cents; Beds 15 cents;* and *Baths 10 cents (clean water extra!)*

TUMBLEWEEDS

Did you know tumbleweeds are actually real plants that detach themselves from their roots and roll with the wind to spread their seeds? I bet you didn't! Real tumbleweeds are hard to find (unless you live on a ranch), so let's make our own:

- Light brown yarn or string
- Balloons
- White glue
- Newspaper
- Clothespins

The tumbleweeds require 20 three-foot pieces of yarn each. Cover your table with newspaper. Mix a bowl of equal parts white glue and water. Inflate the balloons. Hold a piece of yarn by one end, dip it into the glue mixture, and then wrap it around the balloon. Repeat with the rest of the yarn pieces, overlapping and tucking in loose ends until the balloon is covered. Hang the balloons by the tied end with clothespins to dry overnight. (The bathtub is a good place to do this.) When they're dry, carefully pop and remove the balloons. Viola! Instant tumbleweeds!

TABLE COVERS

Red and white gingham or checkered tablecloths are great for a Wild West Party. You can usually find the inexpensive, flannel-backed-vinyl type at the superstore. If not, check the local fabric shop. Most sell the same flannel-backed-vinyl by the yard. You'll have to cut it to the size of the tables, but the cloths can be wiped clean, and easily reused for backyard BBQs and picnics. (I reuse them as drop cloths for small painting projects.) If red and white checkers aren't your style, use a few yards of burlap to cover the tables and snack buffet. Accent the tops with diagonally placed red bandanas.

COOL TIP!

If you're having the party outside or in the garage, add tin pails of peanuts in the shell to each table. Let the cowpokes drop their peanut shells on the floor. They'll love being able to make a mess! After the party, when the Birthday Kid is vacuuming up rogue pieces of straw, point him in the direction of the peanut shells.

POKER CHIPS & CARDS

All real cowboys play poker. So, scatter some cards and poker chips on the tables and around the snack buffet. Lay out a few winning poker hands around the Party Room. Award a prize to the Cowpoke that locates the best hand!

SET THE TONE WITH MUSIC!

Pop in your favorite country CD, or make a new play-list with a mix of old school Roy Rogers, Willie Nelson, Johnny Cash music, and freight train sounds to play in the background of your cool party.

INSTANT CACTI

Did you know it takes about 15 years for a cactus to grow one foot? You won't have time to grow your own for the party, so let's make some!

- Several terra cotta pots (no drainage holes)
- Clean, dry sand or pea gravel
- Cucumbers, zucchini, or green peppers
- Wooden toothpicks

Fill each pot half way with sand or gravel. Poke toothpicks, about an inch apart, into the sides of the cucumbers or zucchini. Turn the green peppers upside down, and add toothpicks starting with the bottom. Make sure your *needles* go all the way around. When you're finished, place your *cactus* in the sand, in the center of a pot. Use a cup to pour more sand or gravel into the pot. (The toothpicks below the sand will help keep the cactus from falling over.) Group several sizes or types of cactus into the same pot, or make your *cacti* different sizes by cutting them in half before adding needles. Place the instant cacti around the Party Room and on the snack buffet. These also make a great party craft activity. (See Activities Section)

COOL IDEA!

Use a watermelon and a very large pot! When it's time for a snack, let the kids remove the *needles,* then slice it up for them.

IF THE PARTY RUNS LATE, MAKE A CITY FOLK CAMPFIRE!

If you don't have the desire or ability to dig your own campfire, a store-bought fire pit will work just fine. Check your local superstore or home improvement center. Fire pits can be used on grass or concrete, but as with real campfire, be sure the surrounding area is flat and clear of leaves and debris.

ABOUT CAMPFIRES:
- Don't use gasoline or lighter fluid to start the fire. Paper works just dandy.
- Don't use store-bought fire starter logs to cook or roast marshmallows. (The chemicals will transfer to your food.)
- Always make sure embers are cool before you leave the area.
- Always keep a working garden hose nearby.
- And most importantly, never leave children unattended near a fire!

OTHER FANCY THINGS TO PONDER...
Rubber barbwire garland; inflatable or jointed cardboard cacti, horses, or cowboys; cotton rope to make lassos; or dried cornstalks make great Wild West decorations.

WILD WEST FOOD

THE GENERAL STORE
Line up a row of glass fishbowls, tie a piece of sisal or raffia around the rims, and fill them with things like beef jerky, individual cheese sticks, pretzel rods, candy root beer barrels, licorice bits, gummy coins, waxed paper taffy, and candy sticks.

CORNBREAD MUFFINS
Grab a few boxes of cornbread muffin mix. Prepare according to the box directions and pour into greased mini-muffin pans. When the muffins are cool, place them in a wicker basket lined with red bandanas.

SOFT PRETZEL LASSOS

- One packet cake yeast
- 4 cups flour
- 1 ½ cups warm water
- 1 ½ tsps sugar
- 3/4 tsp table salt
- One well-beaten egg
- Coarse salt

In a large bowl, dissolve the yeast in the warm water. Add table salt and sugar, and then mix in the flour. Knead the dough until it's smooth and soft. Pull off pieces of dough and roll them into ropes. Form the ropes into *Q* shapes and place on a non-stick cookie sheet. Brush each lasso with beaten egg and sprinkle with coarse salt. Bake at 350 until golden brown. Serve with melted Velveeta cheese or mustard. The easy treats can be formed into all sorts of fun shapes like horseshoes, letter, and numbers.

BBQ'd BURGERS, DOGS, OR BIRD

Cowboys love anything barbequed, but unless you have plenty of help around, don't try to grill during the party. BBQ in the morning, cover with foil, and keep warm in the oven until the guests arrive. (Not all cowpokes like barbeque sauce, so make some without.)

FRESH STRAWBERRIES

If the season is right, pick up a few quarts of strawberries. The morning of the party, clean and remove the stems. Cut the strawberries in half and toss in a large bowl with sugar. Cover and refrigerate until the party. The sugar will melt, and sweeten the strawberries.

PIGS IN A BLANKET

A cowboy classic! Cut some hotdogs in half. Open a can of refrigerated crescent rolls, and place one-half of a hotdog at the larger end of each crescent triangle. Roll, place on cookie sheet, and bake as directed.

LITTLE SHELLYS

- Cans of refrigerated biscuits
- Hamburger
- BBQ sauce
- Shredded cheese

Brown the hamburger in a skillet, drain, and add BBQ sauce to coat. Flatten biscuits and form them into the cups of a muffin pan. Add a spoonful of hamburger mixture to each cup. Top with shredded cheese. Bake according to biscuit can directions. Serve with macaroni and cheese.

LITTLE DAWGIES

Heat up a bag of cocktail weenies and some BBQ sauce in a snack-size Crock-Pot. Serve with cocktail picks. Easy peasy!

CORN ON THE COB

Place ears of corn on individual pieces of aluminum foil. Add butter, salt, and two ice cubes. Fold foil and secure tightly. Cook on the BBQ pit for about 15 minutes. Turn and rotate often. (The ice cubes will keep the corn from dying out.) Keep warm in the oven until the party. Don't forget the cob holders!

OTHER VITTLES TO CONSIDER...

Franks and beans, fried chicken, sloppy Joes, Cheeseburger Hamburger Helper, baked beans, mac and cheese, potato salad, coleslaw and corn chips.

COOL TIPS!

Serve the grub on disposable aluminum pie plates or in potpie tins. Wrap silverware in red bandanas, or prop spoons and forks in glass Mason jars. You can also use Mason jars to serve drinks. They're inexpensive, re-usable, and available at most superstores or anywhere you can buy canning supplies.

WILD WEST DESSERTS

CACTUS CUPCAKES

Prepare a white cake mix according to box directions. Add green food coloring before pouring the batter into your cupcake pans. Bake as directed and let cool completely. Mix green food coloring into a jar of white frosting. Spoon frosting into a zipper bag and snip the corner with a pair of scissors. Frost the cupcakes in thick lines to look like cactus spines. Use dry chow mein noodles for needles.

BROWNIE S'MORES

- One box of brownie mix
- Ten graham crackers
- 2 ½ cups mini-marshmallows
- Three chocolate bars

Line a 13x9-inch pan with foil, and grease with vegetable oil. Overlap graham cracker pieces in the bottom of the pan. Mix batter according to the box directions. Pour over grahams, and bake as directed. Sprinkle the top with marshmallows and broken chocolate bars. Bake three to five minutes or until marshmallows begin to puff. Break a few leftover graham crackers into pieces, and gently press them into the marshmallows. Let cool and use the foil to remove brownies before cutting.

HORSESHOE COWBOY BISCUITS

While your teenage helper is busying the Cowpokes with an activity, open a few cans of store-bought biscuits, and pre-heat vegetable oil in a shallow skillet. Press your thumb into bottom of each biscuit to form a horseshoe. Use tongs to flip and fry until golden brown. Drain on paper towel and roll in cinnamon and sugar.

OVEN FRIED FRUIT PIES

- 2 cans of large refrigerated biscuits
- 2 cups fruit pie filling (any flavor)
- 2 T sugar
- 2 T melted butter
- ½ tsp cinnamon

Preheat oven to 375. Spray cookie sheets with non-stick cooking spray. Open the cans of biscuits and press them into 5-inch circles. Place two tablespoons of pie filling into the center of each circle. Fold the biscuits in half. Seal the edges closed with a fork, and prick the tops to allow air to escape. Place on a cookie sheet, brush with melted butter. Combine sugar and cinnamon in a small bowl, and sprinkle onto the pies. Bake for 15 to 20 minutes or until golden brown. Let cool before serving.

RATTLESNAKE CAKE

- One yellow cake mix
- Giant Tootsie Rolls
- One can of white frosting
- Red and green food coloring

Prepare cake mix according to the box, and pour into a non-fluted Bundt pan. Bake as directed. Let cool completely and remove from pan. Slice the cake in half to form two *C* shapes. Place them on a serving platter in an *S* shape. Trim the corners off the ends to form a head and body. Microwave Tootsie Rolls until they're soft and pliable (less than ten seconds). While warm, mold two Tootsies together to form a flat-coned rattlesnake tail. Use a butter knife to add ridges. Let cool. Mix red and green food coloring into a can of white frosting until you have the desired snake color. Frost the snake cake using a rubber spatula. Add your Tootsie tail to one end. Use leftover Tootsies to form slanted eyes and a red fruit roll-up for a forked tongue.

FRESH WATERMELON

If the weather is warm, it only makes sense to let the cowpokes enjoy a few slices in the backyard. While you're out there, have a seed-spitting contest!

WILD WEST DRINKS

LEMONADE FIZZIES

Prepare a few cans of frozen lemonade in a large punch bowl. Add a liter of lemon-lime soda. Float fresh cut lemon slices in the bowl. Serve in cool, cowboy boot mugs or Mason jars.

SARSAPARILLA

Serve old-fashioned root beer in brown glass bottles. (Orange or cream soda will work too.) Ice the bottles in an aluminum washtub or 35-gallon plastic storage tote.

COOL TIP!

Teach the cowpokes how to blow across the top of their root beer bottles to make them whistle. The bottles will have a different pitch depending on how much liquid is inside. An empty bottle sounds a lot like a freight train whistle!

WILD WEST INDOOR ACTIVITIES

HORSESHOES

This game is mandatory for any Wild West Party! If you're playing indoors, use toy rings, rubber snakes, or beanbags. Divide the cowpokes into two teams. Place an upside down cowboy hat about ten paces away from where the cowpokes are throwin'. Let the players take turns throwing three rings toward the hat. To keep score in this cowpokes version, award a point for each *horseshoe* that touches or lands in the hat. The team with the most points wins. Let each child have a few turns trying to score. Hand out small prizes or pieces of candy for each bulls-eye.

HOT POTATO

Wrap a raw potato in aluminum foil. Have the cowpokes sit in a circle. Start the music. The potato is passed from player to player while the music plays. When the music stops, the player who has the potato is out. The last cowpoke wins.

COOL TIP!

For a fun twist, have the players play while blindfolded. The cowpokes will have to remember to say their neighbor's name aloud, before passing the potato.

PASS THE LASSO

Divide the cowpokes into two teams, and have the teams stand in two lines, facing each other. Pass out plastic straws for the players to hold in their mouths. The first person in each line placed a pretzel knot on the end of their straw. The object is to pass the pretzel, down the line using only their straw. (Don't poke anyone in the eye.) If someone drops the pretzel, it has to go back to the beginning of the line. The first team to get their pretzel *lasso* to the end of the line wins!

EDIBLE KNOTS

Print some simple knot tying directions from the Internet. Pass out coils of rope licorice to the cowpokes. Have a contest to see which cowpoke can tie three different knots the fastest. Use real cotton rope if you don't want the kids hopped up on sweets.

CATTLE DRIVE

Set up an obstacle course with chairs, boxes, or bales of straw. Use string to mark the path. Blow up several balloons. Divide the players into pairs. Hand a broom to each of the first two players. Place four or five balloons on the floor in front of them. Set a timer. The object is for the players to work as a team to *drive their cattle* through the obstacle course without losing any *cows*.

ROPING BRONCOS

Cover a hula-hoop with rope or 1-inch wide tan ribbon by wrapping it around several times. Use clear packing tape to secure at the beginning and end. When the hula-hoop is completely covered, attach one end of a 12-ft length of rope. During the party, place stuffed or inflatable horses, sheep, and cows about ten paces from the starting line. Have the cowpokes take turns trying to *rope* the animals by tossing the hula-hoop like a Frisbee. If the hoop lands over an animal, the player has to pull the animal toward him slowly with the rope, without the varmint getting away!

WHAT IN TARNATION, IS THAT COWBOY SAYING?

This is a fun guessing game to play with school-aged cowpokes. Before the party, write the saying on the front of index cards, and write the translations on the back. The cowpoke that gets the most right wins. Here's a bunch to get you started:

Are you giving me a bunch of *ballyhoo*? (Telling lies)

Quit your bellyaching! (Complaining)

You got a bee in your bonnet. (Problem)

Those two boys are in *cahoots*! (Partners)

You're hair is all *catawampus*! (Messed up)

Quit dilly-dallying and get your work done! (Playing)

You need to get a wiggle on or we'll be late! (Hurry)

Hobble your lip before someone hears you! (Be quiet!)

Let's mosey over to Big John's house! (Walk)

Put on your mud pipes and let's go! (Boots)

You sure are an odd stick! (Strange person)

You sure are a persnickety eater! (Picky)

Don't step in the prairie pancakes! (Cow patties)

You need to pull your horns! (Settle down)

That was really a tear squeezer! (Sad story)

He ate the whole kit and caboodle! (All of it)

THE HANKY TOSS

Have the cowpokes form a line, side by side. Hand each cowpoke a bandana. When you say *go*, the cowpokes must toss the bandana as far they can. They can wad it, roll it, or fold it before they throw it. See whose goes the farthest!

OTHER FUN INDOOR ACTIVITIES TO PONDER...

Velcro darts, checkers, Yahtzee, or card games like I Doubt It, Crazy Eights, or Poker (see Slumber Party Activities). Pick up a kid's Square Dancing or Line Dancing DVD; even little ones will enjoy trying to copy the moves.

WILD WEST OUTDOOR ACTIVITIES

PAN FOR GOLD

Before the party, find some quarter-size rocks, and paint them with gold spray paint. (To make it easier, toss the rocks into a shoebox; spray them; shake the box so the rocks roll over; and spray them again.) Fill a sandbox or kiddie pool with dry sand. Bury the dry *gold* in the sand. Punch holes into several aluminum pie tins with a Phillips screwdriver. During the party, pass out the pie plates, and let the cowpokes sift through the sand to find the loot! Make a time limit and see who can find the most in a minute or two. If you don't have time to paint rocks, just use pennies!

SACK RACES

Use masking tape or string to mark a starting line and a finish line about 30 paces apart. Have the cowpokes form a line, side-by-side at the starting line. Pass out burlap sacks (or trash bags). When you say *go*, the players must jump into their sacks and hop down to the finish line, holding their sack up around their waists. The first to cross the finish line wins!

RATTLESNAKE RODEO

Tie a baby rattle or toy maraca to either end of a 12-ft rope. Have two cowpokes or teenage helpers hold the ends, and whisk it back and forth along the ground. The cowpokes must jump over the *rattling snake* without being bit. For older cowpokes, raise the rope off the ground several inches. See who can jump the longest without being bitten.

HORSESHOES

Hammer a stake into the ground about ten paces from the starting line. Divide the cowpokes into two teams. Let the players take turns throwing three horseshoes towards the stake. (Make sure the other cowpokes are standing well out of the way.) To keep score in this cowpokes version, award a point for each horseshoe that touches or bounces off the stake. The team with the most points wins. You can also play a similar game with 3-inch metal washers. Don't forget to hand out small prizes or pieces of candy for each bulls-eye!

SEED SPITTING CONTEST

Have the cowpokes form a line, side-by-side. Pass out cups full of sunflower or watermelon seeds. Let the players take turns spitting a seed as far as possible. Use a few metal coffee cans for spittoons or targets.

WATER GUN SHOWDOWN

Divide the cowpokes into two teams. Have the players stand in two lines, back-to-back. As you count to ten, each player takes ten steps forward and stops. When you say, *draw*, the players turn around, and squirt their guns at someone in the other group. Any two players squirting their guns at each other are out. .

SHARP SHOOTER

Set up lightweight plastic bottles or empty soda cans on a fence or table, and let the players shoot them off with squirt guns. Easy peasy!

CLANKING COWBELLS

Attach several cowbells (from the craft store) to shoestrings to make two cowbell necklaces. Fill two buckets with watered-down powdered milk, and place a soup ladle into each bucket. Place two, empty glass (or plastic) milk bottles 25 feet away from the buckets. Divide the cowpokes into two teams. Put a cowbell necklace on the first player from each team. When you say *go*, the players must fill their ladles with milk, quickly walk over to pour the milk into the bottle, and return to pass their necklace off to the next player on their team. If the cowbells clank at any time, that player must stop and *moo*, before continuing. The first team to fill their milk bottle wins!

WILD WEST CRAFTS

PIE PLATE SUN CATCHERS

- Aluminum pie tins
- Bath towels
- Pushpins
- Printed shapes
- String or twine

Draw simple western shapes like cacti, sheriff badges, cowboy hats, or boots on plain white paper. Cut the shapes out in circles, so they are the same size as the center of the pie tins. Give each cowpoke a folded bath towel to use as a cushion when poking holes. Let the cowpokes choose a design to masking tape in the middle of their tin. Demonstrate how to punch holes with pushpins, through the paper and the aluminum, every one-half inch, along the outline of the design. When the outline is complete, remove the paper and add a length of string or twine at the top of each plate for hanging. (Check the tins for sharp edges around the holes.)

CORK HORSES

- Large corks
- Medium corks
- Small corks
- Toothpicks
- White glue
- Brown yarn

Pass out supplies to each cowpoke. Demonstrate how to stick a toothpick into the small end of a large cork, angled down for a tail. Add another toothpick at the large end, angled up for a neck. Attach the side of a medium cork for the head. Glue pieces of yarn on the toothpicks for the mane and tail. Add four toothpick legs and four small corks hooves. Make eyes with a permanent black marker.

LEATHER BOOKMARKS

- 1/8-inch thick craft leather
- Leather or plastic lacing
- Pony beads
- Thin-tipped markers
- Hole-punch

Each bookmark will need a piece of craft leather 6 ½ x 2 ½ inches. Pass out strips of leather for the cowpokes to decorate with markers. Demonstrate how to add things like, names, cactus, cowboy hats, stars, etc. (The markers will show much darker on the leather.) Once the bookmarks are decorated, use a sharp hole-punch to add a hole in the top of each one. Fold a length of lacing in half, and thread the loop through the hole. Thread the two ends through the loop, and pull tightly to snug the lacing against the bookmark. Add pony beads and tie a knot to secure.

INSTANT CACTI

- 4-inch, unglazed terra cotta pots
- Clean pea gravel (Sand is messy!)
- Cucumbers or zucchini (cut in half)
- Wooden toothpicks
- Western stickers
- Googly eyes
- Hot glue gun
- Marker

Give each cowpoke a pot to decorate with stickers and markers. When they're finished, pass out some paper plates, wooden toothpicks, and cucumbers. Demonstrate how to poke toothpicks into the *cactus*, so that they stick out about one inch. Leave room on each cucumber to add a face. Pour a bit of pea gravel into the bottom of each pot. Place the cacti in the pots, and pour in more pea gravel. Use a hot glue gun to attach googly eyes, and add a mustache with a permanent marker.

LASSO PENCIL CUPS

- Empty frozen juice cans, baby food jars, or Mason jars
- Several balls of thin brown twine, rope, or yarn
- Hot glue gun

Add a dab of hot glue to secure the end of the twine to the bottom of the side of the container. Let the cowpokes wind the twine around and around, making sure the rows are flat and close together. If you did it right, you won't be able to see the container anymore. Add another dab of hot glue to secure the end of the twine.

HOBBY HORSES

- Men's tan, brown, or black socks
- Tan, brown or black yarn
- 1-inch diameter wooden dowel rods
- Cotton balls or pillow stuffing
- Thick and thin rubber bands
- Large googly eyes
- Hot glue gun
- Small, black, plastic zip ties
- Scissors

Pack stuffing into the foot of a sock until it's solid. Wrap a thick rubber band around a dowel, about 12 inches from the end. Insert that end into the sock, far enough to reach the heel. Stuff more cotton around the dowel in the leg portion of the sock until it's packed, leaving a few inches at the opening. Stretch the rubber band around the opening. Pinch a small section on either side of the heel, and wrap with thin rubber bands to make ears. Between the ears, feed a zip tie into the sock and back out. Lay 12 eight-inch pieces of yarn between the ends of the zip tie, and zip closed. Trim the ends with scissors, and use a hot glue gun to attach googly eyes.

CHAPTER 3
THE COMPLETE GUIDE TO A GROSS PARTY

What kid doesn't love gross stuff? If you're squeamish, then this party is not for you. But, if you think you can handle all of the slime and goo, put on an apron and dig in!

GROSS INVITES!

JARS OF TOXIC WASTE

Prepare a box of green gelatin according to directions. When the gelatin sets, mix in rubber worms and bugs, hairballs from your hairbrush, *press-on* fake fingernails, etc. Refrigerate to set, and then spoon into baby food jars. Secure the lids with clear packing tape. Attach Invite Tags with dirty old shoelaces. These also make a great party craft activity. (See Activities Section)

BARF BAGS

Airsickness bags are easy to find at any medical supply store or online. Print your Invites on Pepto-pink or slime green cardstock. Cut them out with wavy scissors, and add fingerprints, drips, and smears of ketchup, mustard, or chocolate syrup. Pop them inside the bags. Tell the kids to bring their Barf Bag to the party, just in case!

INCONSPICUOUS BROWN BAGS

Write your Invites on the outside of ordinary brown paper lunch bags with a permanent marker. Crumple the bags, and toss a lump of plastic poop into each one! There is a disturbingly large variety of artificial doggie-doo available online. Hand deliver these Gross Invites to catch the reaction of each guest as they peer inside their bag!

Here's an example of how you might word your Gross Party Invite:

> *Boogers, barf, scabs and poo...*
> *We're having a GROSS PARTY and inviting you!*
> *So, put on some old clothes and hold down your lunch.*
> *We'll play icky games and drink Toe Jam punch!*
> *Join the disgusting fun on March 1 from 1-5 pm*
> *At Andrew's house - 7735 Main Street*
> *RSVP (for chickens only!) 555-5555*

GROSS PARTY FAVORS!

Sticky lizards, squishy balls, tubs of slime, fake bugs, worms and spiders, fake poo and vomit, plastic eyeball goblets, and candy plungers make great Gross Party favors. How about some real bug lollipops? Yuck!

FAVOR BAGS

Toss a bunch of old tube socks into the kitchen sink with one-half box of gray clothes dye. Let them soak until they are nice and grungy. Rinse and pop into the dryer. Add your treats and tie the socks in a knot!

GROSS DECORATIONS!

RUBBER ROACHES & BUGS
Scatter these little guys on your doorstep, in corners of the kitchen or Party Room, and in the bathroom. Remember where you put them; you don't want to find them a month later between your couch cushions. Ack!

GROSS GAUZE
Smear ketchup or chocolate syrup on several rolls of dry medical gauze from the dollar store. Drape them on your bushes, shrubs, and mailbox. Soak several unraveled rolls of gauze in the kitchen sink with hot water, and tea bags to make them look used. Rinse and pop in the dryer, and then hang the rolls around the Party Room like streamers.

PLASTIC POO AND VOMIT
What could be grosser? Again, there is variety of these *presents* available online. Look for sites that sell them in bulk, or by the dozen. Strategically place them on your sidewalk and porch. Add a few appropriate puddles to the snack buffet, or rinse them off and float them in your punch bowl!

DIRTY UNDER THINGS
Okay, not literally! When you're soaking your sink full of favor-bag tube socks, toss in some clean, worn out t-shirts, socks, and men's tighty-whities. (If you have a husband, this is the perfect opportunity to get rid of his grungy t-shirts from college.) Hang them with clothespins on a clothesline above the snack buffet. Only boys are gross, so don't hang anything girly. If this idea completely skeeves you out, tone it down by just using new t-shirts and socks from the dollar store.

FAKE BLOOD

Mix red food coloring into a bowl of water. Add a bit of cornstarch to thicken, and stir well. Use this gross mixture to fill plastic test tubes, soak gauze pads and bandages, or drip on the white party plates and napkins. (Fake blood will stain. Let it dry completely, and be sure to secure test tube caps with strips of clear packing tape.)

GIANT USED COTTON SWABS FOR THE YARD

- Two broom handles
- White and yellow spray paint
- Rolls of medical gauze
- Paper towels
- Rubber bands

Cut the broom handles into three even pieces, and spray with white spray paint. Let dry, and wrap paper towels around one end of each piece. Secure with rubber bands. Tightly wrap a layer of medical gauze, forming a cotton swab end. Spray the tops with yellow spray paint to make them nice and *waxy*. Let the paint dry, and use a rubber mallet to insert them into the ground along your driveway or sidewalk! Oh, how the neighbors will love you!

PUDDING BALLOONS

Inflate orange and green balloons with helium. Make a box of chocolate pudding and use your hands to smear a thin layer all over each balloon. The Birthday Kid will love helping with this project! Let the balloons dry and tie them around the Party Room.

SPIDER WEBS

You can gross-out an entire room with just a few bags of fake web. Pull out wispy strands and hang them from doorways, ceiling fans, lamps, and furniture. Don't forget the spiders!

TABLE COVERS

Use black trash bags, brown paper grocery bags, or dig through your linen closet for old sheets and ratty towels. (You know the ones that you feel guilty throwing away, but keep for years, just in case every new sheet and towel that you own gets dirty in a freak linen-closet mishap!) You can also, scour the clearance tables at the fabric store for tan or gray fabric remnants. It doesn't matter what type of fabric you buy, as long as it's gross looking. When you get home, use a pair of scissors to haphazardly rip or trim the edges.

GROSS FOOD!

FISH BOWL BUFFET

Line up several glass fishbowls and fill them with gummy worms and eyeballs, multi-colored cheddar goldfish, pretzels rods, grapes, carrot sticks, or mini-marshmallows.

CHEESY MICE

Scoop a spoonful of spreadable cheese into your palm. Shape it like into a tiny mouse with a pointy nose and a rounded backside. Press two almond slivers into the pointed end for ears. Chop a raisin into tiny pieces and add the pieces for eyes and a nose. Use a curly Chow Mein noodle for a tail. Place the little rodents on top of crackers to serve.

CATERPILLAR COCOONS

All kids love this quick easy meal! Open a few cans of refrigerated crescent rolls. Pre-heat the oven according to directions. Cut hot dogs in half, and place them at the larger end of the crescent triangles. Roll closed, place on a cookie sheet, and bake as directed.

BARF DIP

Combine equal parts sour cream, cream cheese, and salsa in a bowl. Serve with corn chips. (It really does look like barf!)

BBQ'D FINGERS

Heat up a bag of cocktail weenies and BBQ sauce in a snack-size Crock-Pot. Serve with cocktail picks. Easy peasy!

FROZEN EYEBALLS

Clean and de-stem a few bunches of red, green, and black seedless grapes. Freeze them in a plastic zipper bag overnight. Before the party, pour the frozen grapes into a glass fishbowl and add sparkling white grape juice. Serve in clear plastic cocktail cups with a soup ladle.

STICKY BOOGERS

Melt a block of Velveeta in a snack-size Crock-Pot or fondue pot. Stir in a few drops of green food coloring. Serve with pretzel rods.

OCTOPUS SANDWICHES

Slice some hot dogs down the middle with a sharp knife. Lay each half flat and slice again, so you have four long *legs*. Cook the *legs* in shallow frying pan. (They will curl while cooking.) Stuff them into dollar roll buns and top with shredded lettuce.

WORMY BURGERS

Boil some spaghetti noodles until tender. Strain, let cool, and chop into two-inch pieces. In a large bowl, combine raw ground beef or turkey with the chopped noodles. Mix well and form into small patties. Grill or broil as usual, and serve on dollar rolls.

GOLDFISH GUTS

Pour several cans or jars of Mandarin oranges into a glass fishbowl. Add watered-down orange juice. Serve in clear plastic cocktail cups with a soup ladle.

USED COTTON SWAB SNACKS

Pick up some lollipop sticks at your local craft store. Add a mini-marshmallow to each end, and dip in creamy peanut butter. Serve them in an empty cotton swab box!

PUKE PIZZAS

- 3-inch cocktail rye
- 1 pound of Velveeta
- 1 pound of pork sausage
- 1 cup of ketchup

The day before the party, brown the sausage in a skillet and drain. Return to skillet and add cubed Velveeta and ketchup. Cook on low heat until Velveeta is melted. Stir frequently. Arrange cocktail bread on waxed paper. Top each slice of bread with a spoonful of Velveeta mixture. Let cool completely, and stack in a plastic gallon-size zipper bag. Freeze overnight. When you're ready to serve, preheat the oven to 325. Place the pizzas on cookie sheets. Bake 15-20 minutes or until bread is toasted. (These will keep in the freezer for up to a month.) When you're ready to serve, bake in a 325 degrees oven until toasted.

GROSS DESSERTS!

MUD CUPS

Easy peasy! Remove the lids from chilled chocolate pudding cups. Crush some Oreo cookies in a plastic zipper bag and spoon on top of pudding. Add a dollop of whipped topping and a gummy worm to each. (These are also great to serve frozen.)

ARMPIT FUDGE Yep, that's what it's called!

- Powdered sugar
- Cocoa powder
- Butter
- Cream cheese

Before the party, add 1/2 cup powdered sugar and 2 tsps of cocoa powder to several zipper sandwich bags. When it's time for dessert, add 1 T butter and 2 tsp of cream cheese to each bag. Squeeze out the air and zip the bags closed. Hand a bag to each child. Show the kids how to smoosh the bags (under their arms!) until all the ingredients are mixed well. Add things like raisins, peanut butter chips, nuts or mini-M&Ms, and eat out of the bags with spoons.

SWAMP GUNK

Make some green gelatin according to package directions. Arrange plastic cocktail cups on a cookie sheet, and fill the cups half way with gelatin. Refrigerate. Remove from refrigerator when the gelatin starts to solidify and add gummy fish or bugs. Use a hand mixer to beat the remaining gelatin until frothy, add to each cup, and return to refrigerator to set.

CHICKEN POX PANCAKES

- Pancake mix
- Strawberries
- Powdered sugar
- Granulated sugar

They're not just for breakfast anymore! The night before the party, dice strawberries into small pea-size pieces, and put them in a plastic bowl. Sprinkle with granulated sugar, cover with plastic, and refrigerate for two hours. Mix up a batch of pancake batter. Drain the liquid from the strawberry bowl and fold them into the batter. Use a hot griddle to make small pancakes. Let the pancakes cool completely, put them in a plastic zipper bag, and refrigerate until the party. About 30 minutes before your ready to serve, preheat your oven to 300. Spread the pancakes out on a cookie sheet and pop in the oven until warm. Place a few on each small plate and sprinkle with powdered sugar.

MUDDY SNOWBALL COOKIES

- 4 cups flour
- 1 lb butter, softened
- ¾ cup powdered sugar
- 2 tsp vanilla
- Powdered sugar
- Unsweetened cocoa powder

Preheat oven to 375. In a large bowl, use a fork to blend butter, powdered sugar, and vanilla. Slowly mix in the flour. Use your hands to work the mixture into stiff dough. Roll into 1-inch balls. Bake on an ungreased cookie sheet for 15-20 minutes. Let cool on a wire rack. Add ½ cup powdered sugar and 3 T cocoa to a small bowl. Roll each cookie in the *mud*.

KITTY LITTER CAKE This is so incredibly gross!

- One white cake mix
- One box of vanilla pudding mix
- One pkg of shortbread cookies
- Green food coloring
- Small Tootsie Rolls
- One new kitty litter box
- One new pooper-scooper

Prepare the cake mix according to directions. While the cake is baking, prepare the pudding and refrigerate. Put the cookies into a gallon-size plastic zipper bag, and crush with a rolling pin. Separate one-quarter cup of cookie crumbs into a bowl and add a few drops green food coloring. Mix with fork and set aside. Once the cake is cool, crumble it into the kitty litter box, and fold in the chilled pudding. (Mix in just enough to moisten.) Microwave unwrapped Tootsie rolls on a paper plate until pliable. Shape ends so they are no longer blunt, then bury in the mixture. Smooth top with a rubber spatula. Sprinkle a layer of plain crumbled cookies over the top of the mixture. Add a layer of green cookie crumbs. Microwave more Tootsie rolls to add as fresh kitty *presents* to the top. Place the box on newspaper and serve with the pooper-scooper.

MOOSE POOP

Place three or four pieces of caramel corn into each cup of a non-stick mini-muffin pan. Melt broken chocolate bars or kisses in the microwave, 20 seconds at a time. (Be careful not to over-heat. The chocolate will get crumbly.) Spoon the mixture over the caramel corn. Refrigerate until cool. Sprinkle with powdered sugar.

GROSS DRINKS!

TOE JAM PUNCH

In a punch bowl, mix one can of frozen lemonade with two liters of lemon-lime soda. Add one-half gallon of rainbow sherbet. The sherbet will melt and turn the mixture grayish-brown. Yuk!

SPIT WAD SODAS

Call around to your local grocery stores to see which one carries frozen ice cream beads (a.k.a. Dippin' Dots). They're out there; you just have to look. When you're ready to serve, pour into clear plastic cocktail cups and cover with root beer. Try different flavor combinations: chocolate with strawberry soda, vanilla with cola, or banana split with cream soda.

GROSS INDOOR ACTIVITIES!

SLIMY SPELLING BEE

Divide the players into teams of two. Hand each team an empty paper plate, and a plate full of alphabet soup. Each team must dig through the soup to spell words on the empty plate with the noodle letters. Set a timer for two minutes and see which team has the *sickest* spellers. Give one point for each letter in the spelled-out words.

THE DIRTY DIAPER SNIFF

Fill eight baby diapers with eight different flavors of baby foods like applesauce, squash, carrots, etc. Number each diaper one through eight. Pass out index cards and pencils. Instruct the players to sniff each diaper, and then, write down what they think the baby had for lunch! The player with the most right answers wins!

COOL TIP!

You can also play this game with brown lunch bags, and gross ingredients like onions, parmesan cheese, green peppers, garlic, etc. Don't let the players peek while they're sniffing!

CORNSTARCH CAPERS

Empty 4 cups of cornstarch into a bowl, and stir with a wooden spoon, while you add up to 2 cups of water. The mixture needs to be the consistency of thick pancake batter. Let one child slowly stick their hand into the mixture, and slowly pull it out. (It's covered with goo!) Let another child smack the mixture with a flat hand. (The mixture becomes a solid like gelatin!) Now let one child grab a handful of the mixture, and roll it between their palms. As long as they're rolling, a ball will form; when they stop, the ball disappears!

GROSS OUTDOOR ACTIVITIES!

WARNING!

All of the activities on the following few pages are extremely gross! Make sure you remind the kids to bring swimsuits or old clothes to the party, and have a garden hose available to rinse off before they go home!

POPPIN' ZITS

Fill red balloons with canned whip cream and scatter them around the yard. When you say, *go*, the players choose a balloon and try to pop it without using their hands. They can sit on it, stomp on it, or lay on it. Whoever pops the most, wins!

SPAGHETTI AND MEATBALL RELAY

- Two old pair of boots or galoshes
- Four aluminum pie tins
- Pre-cooked meatballs
- Spaghetti noodles
- Spaghetti sauce
- Vegetable oil
- Goggles

Before the party, cook and drain the spaghetti noodles. Toss with vegetable oil, and put a handful of noodles into each boot. During the party, place two empty pie tins and a pair of spaghetti boots on a starting line. Twenty paces away, place two pie tins filled with sauce and meatballs. Divide the players into two teams, and have each team line up behind a pair of spaghetti boots. When you say *go*, the first player from each team puts on their goggles, squishes their feet into the boots, runs to the other end, and picks up a meatball, (using only their mouth), runs back to the starting line, drops the meatball into the empty tin, slips out of the boots, and tags the next player on their team. The next players repeat the process until all meatballs are moved. The quickest team wins!

PUDDING FLING

Have the players sit in two rows facing one another. Pass out goggles, chocolate pudding cups, and plastic spoons. When you say *go*, the players bend their plastic spoons to fling pudding at their partners. The partners must try to catch the pudding in their mouths! Make sure to have your digital or video camera handy. There's no real winner in this game; it's just good old fashioned gross fun!

WORM HUNT

Arrange paper plates around the picnic table. Place one gummy worm in the center of each plate, and cover it with whipped topping. Have the players stand in front of their plates, with their hands behind their backs. When you say *go*, the players dive into their plates with their faces, to hunt for worms under the whipped topping. Let the first three to finish face-off for grand champion.

PUKED ON PIGGIES

- Two plastic dish tubs
- Several cans of creamed corn
- One folding chair
- Ten marbles

Place a tub full of creamed corn in front of a folding chair, and toss in ten marbles. (Add ketchup to make it more *vomit-y!*) The object of the game is for each barefoot player to find and remove the marbles using only their toes. The quickest foot wins! (Fill the second dish tub with plain water so the players can rinse their piggies.)

MARSHMALLOW WARS

Mark two borders, 15 feet apart using masking tape or string. Divide the players into two teams. Have the players stand on their borders with buckets of *grenades* (marshmallows covered in pancake syrup). Set a timer for two minutes, and let the attack begin! The players can throw back any grenades that land on them or over their borders. When time is up, whichever team has the least grenades on their side of the border, wins!

SKUNK WARS

Have the players stand in a circle. Pass out goggles to the players, and tell them to put them on and close their eyes. When the players eyes are closed, place several cans of whipping topping in the middle of the circle. Now, get as far away as possible, grab your camera and yell *GO*! Let the players run around trying to spray each other like skunks!

GROSS CRAFTS!

FLUBBER

BOWL A - ¾-cup water, 1-cup white glue, and green food coloring

BOWL B - ½-cup water, 2 tsp of Borax laundry powder.

When the kids are around, pour the first bowl into the second bowl. No need to stir, just reach in, and pull out a glob of Flubber!

JARS OF TOXIC WASTE

- One box of clear, unflavored gelatin
- One box of green gelatin
- Baby food or Mason jars (leftover from the Dirty Diaper Sniff)
- Gross ingredients: rubber bugs, hairballs, *press-on* fake fingernails, cotton swabs, small band-aids, etc.

The morning of the party, combine and prepare the two boxes of gelatin. Refrigerate. During the party, spoon some gelatin into each jar, and pass them out to the kids. Demonstrate how to add the *toxic* ingredients. Use spoons to arrange the gunk in the jars, and secure the lids with clear packing tape for the ride home.

DRYER LINT CLAY

- 6 cups firmly packed dryer lint
- 1 cup of warm water
- 1 cup of white glue
- 3 T dishwashing liquid

Mix all of the ingredients together in a large bowl. When the mixture becomes firm, knead it with your hands until smooth. Pass out pieces of waxed paper and chunks of linty clay. Demonstrate how to form it into shapes or small bowls. Send the creations home in a shoebox or plastic cup. They will take several days to dry completely. (If the party is in April or May, make mom a gross, linty jewelry dish for Mother's Day!)

FAKE POO

Even if you have plenty of these little *presents* around the Party Room, the kids will love making their own to take home. Pick up a bucket of brown no-bake, modeling clay at the craft store. Show the kids how to roll a chunk of clay between their palms to form a snake. Coil the snake into a pile of disgusting poo. Add peanuts, un-popped popcorn, and pipe-cleaner flies! Let dry according to the package instructions.

50

CHAPTER 4

THE COMPLETE GUIDE TO AN UNDER THE SEA PARTY!

Planning an Under the Sea Party is as easy as 1-2-3! Decorations and supplies are available everywhere, and if you (or your friends) have a pool, you will be well on your way!

UNDER THE SEA INVITES

SOMETHING FISHY
Fill baby food jars with cheddar goldfish, gummy fish, or sharks. Tie blue ribbon around the caps, and cut the Invite Tags into shapes like fish, whales, or shark fins.

SENDING OUT AN SOS
Did you know that SOS is not an acronym for "save our ship" or "save our soul"? SOS is actually a "backronym", which means SOS came first, and the familiar words were chosen to fit later. Cool! Now that you feel smarter, remove the labels from several empty water bottles. Add handfuls of sand and seashells to each bottle. Roll up your Invites and place them inside the bottles. Tie pieces of sisal or raffia around the rims, and deliver your cool backronyms!

OCEAN GLOBES

Design Your Own Snow Globe kits are available online for a few dollars each. Most are designed so that you can insert a photo (or in this case an Invite) as a background to the watery scene. Follow the directions on the packages, and fill the globes with water, blue food coloring, sand, and tiny seashells. If the kits come with artificial snowflakes, substitute clear or silver glitter. Pass the globes out to your invited guests. Then, at the party, take pictures of each kid having fun. Print the photos, and include them with the Thank You notes, along with instructions for how to replace the Invites in the globes with party pictures. What a fun keepsake!

Here's an example of how you might word your Under the Sea Party Invite:

> **Come; join my adventure under the sea...**
> **Down where the fishes swim wild and free!**
> **We've planned a birthday that's sure to be grand...**
> **With silly games and treats, you won't find on land!**
> **The celebration begins April 25 at TWO**
> **Hope you dive in, we'll be waiting for you!**
> **Nick's house - 7735 Main Street R.S.V.P. 555-5555**

UNDER THE SEA FAVORS

Fish and shark squirters, bubbles, sunglasses, seashell whistles, fish-shaped straws, and shark tooth necklaces. Any sea-worthy treat will do!

FAVOR BAGS

Use plastic sand buckets from the dollar store as favor bags. At the end of the party, add your decorative seashells and plastic marine animals to the buckets.

REAL FISH FAVORS

Borrow a 10-gallon fish tank from a neighbor or friend. Fill with room temperature water. The morning of the party, have your husband pick up individual bags of live goldfish from the pet store. Float the bags in the fish tank during the party. When it's time to go, let each kid choose a bagged fish to take home! Make care packages by filling small, quart-size fishbowls with handfuls of aquarium rocks, small baggies of fish food, and care instructions.

NOTE: Don't release the fish into the aquarium; leave them in the baggies provided by the pet store for the trip home. (Also, it's a good idea to give the other parents a heads up that you plan to send each kid home with a new friend!)

UNDER THE SEA DECORATIONS

STREAMERS
Pick up several rolls of blue and green paper streamers. Cut them into varying lengths, and hang from the ceiling with poster putty. If you don't have the time or energy to do the entire ceiling, just fill in a circle in the center of the room, or hang two columns of streamers on either side of the snack buffet. Use a stapler to attach paper clown fish or starfish to the streamers.

HELIUM BALLOONS
I always say, the more the better when you're talking balloons! Blue and green make for great Under the Sea colors. Or try tying several clear, air-filled balloons together with fishing line. Hang them in columns to look like bubbles rising from the sea floor!

CORAL REEF
Make your own coral reef by spray-painting crumpled newspaper, large rocks, and inexpensive natural or loofa sponges (from the Beauty Dept.) with neon-colored spray paint. Use a black light to highlight your reef. Add schools of three-dimensional fish by poking toothpicks into the bottom of gummy fish, and inserting them along a sea sponge!

TABLE COVERS
Cover the tables with blue shimmering fabric, or inexpensive burlap from the fabric store. Top with fishing nets, seashells, rocks, and plastic crabs or lobsters.

SAND, SEASHELLS & CRABS

Crush a few boxes of vanilla wafers to make your own sand, or pick up a bag of real sand at the hardware store. (After the party, have the Birthday Kid clean it up with a shop-vac.) All shapes and sizes of seashells are available at the craft store. If you're near the beach, collect your own, or use the shells you brought home from vacation! Plastic fish, lobsters, and crabs can be bought in bulk online. You will find plenty of ways to use them, or give them away as favors.

TREASURE CHEST

Plastic and cardboard pre-made treasure chests are easy enough to find, but if you want to get your kids in on the action, make your own!

- Cardboard box or Styrofoam cooler
- Brown (and gold) craft paint
- Aluminum foil & newspaper
- Glue stick
- 1/4 inch wooden dowel
- Jewels, beads, coins, etc.

Paint the box or cooler with brown craft paint. (Spray paint will melt Styrofoam.) Let it dry completely, and then use a glue stick to attach aluminum foil hinges and latches, or paint them on with gold craft paint. Use a wooden dowel to prop open the lid, and stuff crumpled newspaper into the bottom for filler. Add plastic gold coins, jewels, strings of pearls and beads.

BUBBLES, BUBBLES, BUBBLES

What Under the Sea Party would be complete without tons of bubbles? Set up an electric or wind-powered bubble machine on a high shelf in the Party room. Wind-powered bubble machines are significantly less expensive (under ten dollars online) than electric bubble machines. If you're using one indoors, you will obviously need a small fan to produce the wind.

BLUE MOOD
Pick up some regular blue light bulbs at your local hardware store, and change out some of the bulbs in the Party Room. Close the curtains or cover the windows with dark construction paper to get a cool deep-sea effect.

COOL TIP!
If you want to spend a little more money, set up an *Ocean-in-Room Projector* (under 30 dollars online). This cool projector-speaker gizmo will transform any ordinary room into a shimmering blue, underwater lagoon! After the party, you can turn up the soothing sounds, and put your crabby kids and husband to sleep, or give it to a friend with a baby. Better yet, list it for sale online and get your money back!

UNDER THE SEA FOOD

CORAL REEF SNACK BUFFET
Line up several glass fishbowls. Tie blue or green ribbon around the rims, and fill them with multi-colored cheddar goldfish, grapes, carrot sticks, M&Ms, pretzel goldfish, gummy fish, and sharks.

LOBSTER QUESADILLAS
Use red or orange tomato-basil tortillas, and finely shredded cheese to make quesadillas in a skillet (with butter), or the microwave. Use a lobster-shaped cookie cutter to cut out snack sizes. Stack the quesadillas to cut more than one at a time.

NEMO NIBBLETS
Make layered stacks of American cheese, turkey, Swiss cheese, ham, and another slice of American cheese. Use a sharp knife to slice the stack into nine blocks, and skewer with picks.

OCTOPUS SANDWICHES
Slice hot dogs down the middle with a sharp knife. Lay each half flat and slice again, so you have four long *legs*. Cook the *legs* in shallow frying pan. (They will curl while cooking.) Stuff the fried *legs* into dollar roll buns and top with shredded lettuce.

PEANUT BUTTER & JELLY FISH
Prepare PBJs as usual, on white or wheat bread. Cut the sandwiches with fish-shaped cookie cutters. Easy peasy!

CLAM SANDWICHES
Slice open several dollar rolls, leaving one side hinged, and stuff with filling like tuna salad, ham salad, chicken salad, or egg salad.

SEA SNAILS
Spread cream cheese on room-temperature tortillas. Add slices of roast beef to each, and place a row of sweet pickles on the ends. Roll tightly, starting with the pickle ends. Slice each roll and secure with a cocktail pick.

OTHER SEA-WORTHY SNACKS TO CONSIDER:
Corn chip "scoops" look a lot like chunks of coral. Pretzel rods can double as driftwood. Fish sticks look like, well, fish sticks. Cooked spinach linguini makes great seaweed (serve tossed with butter and parmesan cheese) and of course, shells and cheese!

UNDER THE SEA DESSERTS

SEAWEED
In a saucepan, melt white-chocolate chocolate chips, stirring constantly. Remove from heat and add a few drops of green food coloring. Add dry chow mein noodles or pretzel sticks, and stir until coated. Drop spoonfuls onto waxed paper and let cool.

UNDER THE SEA ADVENTURE CAKE

- One cake mix (any flavor)
- Two cans of white frosting
- Blue food coloring
- Vanilla Wafers
- Candy Sour Straws
- Fruit roll ups
- Candy chocolate rocks
- Gummy fish and sharks

Prepare the cake mix according to directions, and pour into a 13x9 greased cake pan. Bake according to directions. Let the cake cool completely, and invert onto a serving plate. Mix food coloring into three cups of frosting, and frost the cake. Crush vanilla wafers, and spoon onto the bottom third of the cake and sides to make a sandy ocean bottom. Twist sour straws or slices of green fruit roll-ups to make columns of seaweed. Use candy-covered chocolate rocks along the sandy bottom. Add schools of gummy fish and sharks to the middle.

SANDY BEACH CUPS

Peel the lids off several banana or vanilla pudding cups. Sprinkle crushed vanilla wafers on top; add gumballs as beach balls; pop in a cocktail beach umbrella; slice fruit roll-ups or Fruit Stripe gum into rectangles to add as beach towels.

ICE CREAM OCTOPUS

Arrange four green sour candy straws on each plate for arms. Add a scoop of green pistachio ice cream on top for a body. Use different color M&Ms for eyes. Try different flavor combinations: strawberry licorice whips and strawberry ice cream; chocolate licorice and rocky road ice cream; blue licorice and bubblegum ice cream, etc.

AQUARIUM CUPS

Prepare two boxes of blue gelatin according to directions. Refrigerate until slightly thickened. Line up several clear plastic cocktail cups on a cookie sheet. Place a layer of strawberries in the bottom of each cup. Pour thickened gelatin evenly over the fruit. Suspend fruit snacks in the gelatin. Refrigerate about one hour or until firm.

OCTOPOPS

The day before the party, pour equal parts orange juice and cranberry juice into clear plastic cocktail cups that are arranged on a cookie sheet. Drape eight gummy worms around the rim of each cup, making sure that at least half of each worm is submerged in the juice. Carefully move the tray to the freezer for one hour. When the pops are semi-frozen, insert pop-sicle sticks into the center of each cup. Return to the freezer until the party. Remove the octopops from the freezer five minutes before serving. When the kids pull them out of their cups, the worms will dangle down and look like octopus legs.

UNDER THE SEA DRINKS

SHARK PUNCH

A day before the party, make shark cubes by freezing bite-sized gummy sharks in ice cube trays filled with water. The candy will dissolve while freezing and tint the cubes. Pour equal parts of blue fruit punch and lemon-lime soda into a punch bowl. Add your shark cubes as the guests arrive.

SEAWEED WATER

Prepare two cans of frozen apple juice in a clear glass pitcher. Add drops of blue food coloring. Wash a few, new aquarium plants with soap and water and add them to the pitcher before serving.

WHERE THE LAVA MEETS THE SEA DRINKS

Mix three cups of apple juice and two-3 oz. boxes of green gelatin in a saucepan. Heat and stir the mixture until the gelatin dissolves. Remove the saucepan from heat, and stir in another three cups of apple juice. Refrigerate the mixture until thickened. Divide the mixture evenly into 12 plastic cocktail cups. Slowly pour red fruit punch down the side of each cup. The *lava* will float on top of the gelatin. Serve with spoons and straws.

UNDER THE SEA ACTIVITIES

GUPPY, GUPPY, SHARK
Have the players sit in a circle. Let the Birthday Kid be the first fisherman. The fisherman gets to walk around the circle saying, *guppy*, while patting (not hitting) each player on the head. When the fisherman decides to say *shark*, the shark jumps up and runs around the circle trying to tag the fisherman. If the fisherman gets back to the shark's place, the shark must be the new fisherman. If the fisherman is tagged, they have to sit in the middle until another fisherman is tagged.

LAND LUBBERS
Make a line with masking tape or string. Have the players stand behind the line. Let the Birthday Kid call out commands: *land, sea, or air*. If the commander yells, *land*, everyone jumps behind the line. If the commander yells, *sea*, everyone jumps over the line. If the commander yells *air*, everyone jumps straight up. Have the commander yell the commands faster and faster. Anyone who jumps on the line or makes a mistake is out.

FISH STORIES
Have the players sit in a circle. The first player says, *I went fishin' the other day and I caught a* (guppy, shark, whale, dolphin, turtle, cod, catfish, stingray, lobster, crab, etc.) *and it was this big!* (The player demonstrates with his hands how big: arms spread wide, hands apart or between finger and thumb.) The next player says, *Oh yeah, well I went fishin' the other day and I caught* (whatever first player said) *and it was this big* (however big the first player said). *Then, I caught a* (new kind of fish) *and it was this big* (new fish size). The game continues around the circle with each player repeating all of the fish and sizes of the players before, then adding their own. Any player that forgets a fish or size is out.

OCEAN CHARADES

Before the party, fill a fishbowl with paper slips that have the names of ocean creatures. Have the players sit in a circle, and let the Birthday Kid choose a slip out of the bowl. Set a timer. The player has 30 seconds to act like the ocean creature on their slip. They can make sounds, but can't say words! The first person to guess correctly gets to choose a slip and act out a new ocean creature. Play until everyone has a chance to pretend to be a sea creature!

Here's a starter list with acting hints for younger players:
SHARK- A hand fin on the head, mean look, and chomping teeth.
OCTOPUS- A slow wiggly walk, flapping arms, and suction sounds.
WHALE- A deep hum, slow swim, tail flap, and whooshing sound.
DOLPHIN- A big smile, high-pitched dolphin *E*'s, and hand fin.
JELLYFISH- A slow blobby wiggle and zapping sound.
STARFISH- Lie down and slowly pick up each stretched arm and leg.
EEL- Blobby wiggle with arms stuck to the sides and zapping sounds.
SEAHORSE- Holding fake reigns and bobbing head from front to back.
STINGRAY- Belly on the floor, slow arm flaps, and pointy tail.
CRAB- Squat with arms tucked inside knees, and pinching fingers.
SNAIL- Sit with knees tucked in, and wiggly peace sign fingers overhead.
ANGELFISH- Make a snow angel while making fish lips.
BLOWFISH- Sucked in cheeks, puffy cheeks, and finger spikes.

THE CAPTAIN SAYS

Have the players form a line, side-by-side. Choose one player to be the captain. The captain gives orders to the other players to make motions. *The captain says thumbs up. The captain says, hop on one foot. The captain says, hands on your head.* If the captain doesn't say, *the captain says*, the players do not follow the order. Any player who makes the motion is out. The last player gets to be the new captain.

FISH FACE MARATHON

Show the kids how to suck their cheeks in to make fish lips. See who can hold the face the longest without giggling. It's much harder than you think!

CRAB RACES

Use masking tape to mark two goal lines 20 feet apart. Divide the players into two teams. Half of each team lines up behind each goal line. If you can, demonstrate the crab walk (walking on your hands and feet with your belly pointing up). The first player on each team gets into position on one goal line. When you say *go*, the two players crab walk to the other goal line, and tags the next player on their team.

HUNTING SEASHELLS IN THE ABYSS

Did you know that sunlight only penetrates 300 feet into the ocean? Below that, it is pitch black! Let's show the kids what it's like to be a deep-sea diver! Bury seashells in a sandbox or giant washtub filled with dry sand. Blindfold the players, and let them feel around in the sand for shells. Whoever finds the most wins! To make it more challenging, add dry pasta shapes!

UNDER THE SEA CRAFTS

BABY FOOD JAR OCEAN GLOBES

- Empty baby food jars
- Coarse sand
- Clear, iridescent glitter
- Blue food coloring
- Small, assorted seashells
- Hot glue gun

Pour the sand and seashells into separate bowls. Let the kids fill their jars with 1/8 inch of coarse sand, and several seashells. Add a tsp of glitter and several drops of blue food coloring to each, before you fill them with water. Close the lids to the jars and add a bead of glue around the rim to prevent leaks.

TISSUE SEA ANIMALS

- Printed outlines of sea animals
- 1-inch squares of colored tissue paper
- New unsharpened pencils
- White glue

Search the Internet for free printable ocean creatures. Look for simple shapes like fish, octopus, sharks, starfish, and crabs (or draw your own!) Print the pictures on white cardstock. During the party, pour puddles of glue on a few paper plates. Let the kids choose their own design. Demonstrate how to put a piece of tissue over the eraser end of a pencil. Squeeze the tissue so it takes the shape of the eraser, and dip it into the glue. Press the tissue piece onto the design, remove the pencil, and repeat. Use green tissue for an octopus, red tissue for crabs, or blue tissue to make a cool whale. Make eyes with one black tissue surrounded by a row of white tissue. Cut out the shapes, leaving a 1-inch border around each design.

SEASHELL WIND CHIMES

- Several plastic Pringle can lids
- Medium-sized seashells
- A metal awl (or big nail)
- Drill and small drill bit
- Cotton String

If you don't have the patience to drill holes in several dozen seashells, get a bag of pre-drilled shells at you local craft store. Before the party, use an awl to punch six holes around the perimeter of plastic Pringles can lids. During the party, pass out a plastic can lid, and three 24-inch long pieces of cotton string to each kid. Demonstrate how to fold the strings in half, and hold them together by the folded end. Tie all six strings together into one knot, leaving a two-inch loop. Feed the loose end of each string through a hole in the plastic lid. String shells along the length of each string about two inches apart. Tie a knot after each shell to keep it from slipping down. When finished, pick up the wind chime by the loop, and brush your hand to hear the clinking seashell chimes.

PAPER PLATE JELLYFISH

- Paper plates
- Paper streamers
- White glue and stapler
- Scissors
- Markers or glitter glue
- Googly eyes

Cut the paper plates in half before the party. Let the kids decorate the half circle (body) with markers or glitter glue. Let the kids glue googly eyes to their jellyfish, and staple paper streamer strips along the bottom.

STAINED GLASS WAX FISH

- Cardboard & waxed paper
- Black paper
- Pencil sharpeners & a utility knife
- Old crayons
- Low heat iron
- Scissors, glue sticks

The week before the party, draw a simple fish outline (an oval with a triangle tail) on an 8"x10" piece of cardboard. Draw another fish one-half inch inside the outline. Use scissors to cut around the outside, and a utility knife to cut out the center. (You should have a one-half inch wide cardboard frame shaped like a fish.) Use the template to make the same size frames out of black construction paper, two for each child. During the party, cut pieces of waxed paper, (twice the height of the fish frame) and fold them in half. Let the kids use handheld pencil sharpeners to make wax shavings from different colored crayons. (These will be the fish scales.) Sandwich the shavings between the two sides of waxed paper. Cover with a pressing cloth, and melt flat with a low heat iron. (Test the iron to make sure it doesn't melt through the waxed paper.) Use a glue stick to make a wide line around the front of one fish frame. Lay the waxed paper on top. Add glue to the other frame, and lay it onto the top of the waxed paper, lining up the front and back frames. Press firmly. Let the glue dry for a few minutes and use scissors to trim the excess waxed paper from around the edges. Glue large googly eyes in the same place on both sides, and staple a piece of yarn to the top for a hanger. Hang in the stained glass fish in a sunny window!

PAINTED FISH

- Empty water bottles
- Various colors of craft paint
- Long handled paint brushes
- Colored cardstock
- Googly eyes
- Markers
- Hot glue gun
- Newspaper

Before the party, cut various sizes of top fins, tail fins, and side fins out of colored cardstock. Leave a one-half inch tab at the end of each fin, where it will attach to the fish. During the party, cover the table with newspaper. Place several bowls of colored paint in the center, and add a paint brush to each. Hand each child: two side fins, a top fin, and a tail fin to decorate with markers on both sides. When they're finished, set the fins aside and give each child a water bottle. Show them how to use the paint brushes to add colors of paint to the insides of the bottles. When everyone is done, tightly replace the caps and let the kids shake them to spread the paint around inside the bottles. Use a hot glue gun to attach googly eyes, the top fin, and tail fin. Attach the side fins so that the cardstock will keep the bottle from rolling over.

SALT DOUGH SEA CREATURES

BASIC RECIPE:

- 2 cups table salt
- 2 cups flour
- 1 cup water

ADDITIONAL SUPPLIES:

- Waxed paper
- Dixie cups
- Toothpicks
- Thin-tipped markers
- Food coloring
- Ocean-themed cookie cutters

Pre-heat the oven to 300. In a large bowl, mix the salt, water, and flour. Add drops of food coloring. (Prepare separate batches for different colors.) Knead until the dough is smooth. If the dough is too dry, add a bit of water. If it's sticky, add a bit of flour. Give each child a chunk of dough, a piece of waxed paper, a small pile of flour, and a Dixie cup with water.

OPTION #1: (for younger kids)

Roll pieces of dough into 1/8-inch thick patties. Let the kids use the cookie cutters to cut out sea creatures on waxed paper. Demostrate how to use a toothpick to add details like eyes, mouths, fish scales, shark gills, ribs on seashells, and divots to starfish. Use a floured spatula to move the creatures to a baking sheet.

OPTION #2: (for older kids)

Show the kids how to roll the dough between their palms to make shapes like snakes or balls. Make pieces stick together by adding a dab of water. Make sure the edges are smooth and the thicknesses are even to prevent jagged edges.

SEASHELL RELIEF- Pick up small scallop shells at the craft store. Use any color dough to form a round ball. Flatten into a 1-inch disc on floured waxed paper. Press the back of a scallop into the center, careful not to press through.

CRABS- Use red colored dough to form a ball in your palms. Place two 4-inch, red pipe cleaners in the shape of an *X* on floured waxed paper. Press the dough ball onto the center of the *X* and flatten with your palm into a ¼-inch thick disc. Use a toothpick to add eyes on top.

LOBSTERS- Use red colored dough to form a ball in your palms, and then shape it into a long oval. Place it on top of three evenly spaced 4-inch red pipe cleaners. Make a small dough triangle for a tail, and two smaller, pointed oval balls for pinchers. Use a toothpick to poke eyes on the top of your lobster.

Place the creations on a cookie sheet and bake for one hour, or until they are hard and dry to the touch. (If they're not dry all the way through, that's okay.) Let cool for 15 minutes on a wire rack. Highlight details with thin-tipped permanent markers, and add their name and the date. Use a hot glue gun to attach magnets or safety pins to the back of your creatures. (Make sure they're big enough. The dough is somewhat heavy.) Add a clear coat of acrylic spray to make the creations last a lifetime.

CHAPTER 5

THE COMPLETE GUIDE TO A CAMPOUT

Since the dawn of time kids have loved sitting by a fire, and camping out under the stars. There's so much to see and do right in your backyard, so let's plan a cool adventure!

CAMPOUT CONSIDERATIONS...

CAMPFIRES
If you plan to build a campfire, *you absolutely need another adult or teenage helper to assist with the party*. There will be times that you'll need to go inside the house, and you should never leave children unattended around a fire. (See Decorations Section)

SLEEPING OUTSIDE
"How old is old enough to sleep outside?" It really depends on the group of kids. Some are more adventurous; some are more timid. Here are the guidelines I use for the kids in my life:

UNDER AGE 8
Little ones need an adult outside with them the entire night (if anything, to repel the boogieman on the way to the bathroom)! Most of the campers will end up sleeping inside anyway. So be prepared to move the tent, or set up another one in the basement before the party.

AGES 8 TO 12
These kids can usually handle the night without an adult in the immediate vicinity. Nevertheless, I always place a non-negotiable, baby monitor (the plug in type - no batteries) in the tent with them, and I clearly outline the rules and consequences before I head inside.

OVER 13
Teens are more independent and capable of surviving the night alone. That independence often spawns mischief. Rules and consequences need to be repeated loudly, and often; NO leaving the yard. NO fires. NO yelling. NO tree-climbing, etc.

CAMPOUT INVITES

JIFFY POP POPPERS
Do you remember how fun these were when we were kids? They are still available at most larger groceries. Print your Invites on cardstock, cut them out, and attach to the bottom of the poppers with clear packing tape. Make sure to tell your guests to bring their popper to the party. If you can't find the poppers, just tape your Invites to cans of baked beans!

S'MORES MIX
Mix mini-marshmallows, Golden Grahams cereal, and milk-chocolate chocolate chips in a large bowl. Divide the mixture into plastic zipper sandwich bags, baby food jars, or Mason jars. Attach Invite Tag with brass fasteners or ribbon.

Here's an example of how you might word your Campout Invites:

GABI'S BIRTHDAY IS SOON
AND WE'RE SO EXCITED...
WE'RE HAVING A CAMPOUT
AND YOU ARE INVITED!
SO, PACK UP YOUR SLEEPING BAG, FLASHLIGHT AND PILLOW...
YOU CAN BRING YOUR TEDDY BEAR OR PET ARMADILLO!
WE'LL BUILD A REAL CAMPFIRE AND GIGGLE A TON...
HOPE YOU CAN MAKE IT AND JOIN ALL THE FUN!
OCTOBER 13TH 5 PM-10 AM
CAMP PACINO - 7735 MAIN STREET
R.S.V.P. 555-5555

CAMPOUT PARTY FAVORS

You will find a ton of Campout party favors at the dollar store. Look for glow-in-the-dark bugs, whistles, compasses, harmonicas, bandanas, bug catchers, butterfly nets, camo bucket hats, and plastic canteens. The supercenter will have fun favors like twig-shaped pencils, kid binoculars, flashlights, mess kits, and freeze-dried ice cream.

CAMP SHIRTS

This is the most popular Invite Favor I've made for my own kids' parties. Pick up plain t-shirts from the supercenter. Stick to 100% cotton, and buy a size larger than you normally would. Wash the shirts before personalizing; this will take care of any shrinkage. When the shirts are dry, customize each one with the camper's name or nickname, your camp name, and the year. (See next page.) When you're finished, roll them up, and use twine to attach the Invite Tags. Remind your guests to wear their cool shirts to the Campout!

CAMP SHIRT OPTION #1

(Requires the crafting ability of a 13 year old) Pick up some fabric paint, and a 1/4-inch paintbrush at the craft store. Follow the directions on the bottle. Sometimes you'll need to set the paint with an iron, 24 hours after it dries. If you do, place a piece of paper (or pressing cloth) on top of the paint before you iron. This will keep the paint from transferring to your iron.

CAMP SHIRT OPTION #2

(Requires the crafting ability of a ten year old) Iron-on transfer letters are another easy way to personalize the camp shirts. Heat up your iron, follow the package directions, and go to town! Again, make sure you pre-wash the shirts before personalizing.

CAMP SHIRT OPTION #3

(Requires the crafting ability of a five year old) If you can write, you can use fabric markers! Print the camper's name, your camp name, and the year, in small capital letters on the front, where a pocket would be. Practice on a piece of paper before you try it on a shirt. Easy peasy!

HOMEMADE WEENIE ROASTER FAVORS

The week before the party, make a personalized roaster for each camper. Just follow the dough recipe for Salt Dough Critters in the Activities Section. Form the dough into shapes to use as handles on the roasters: a row of four life-size marshmallows, a hotdog in a bun, or a chubby snake! After you've formed the handles, carefully insert straightened wire clothes hangers (or 30-inch long, 1/8-inch diameter metal dowels from the hardware store). The roasters will be too long to dry in the oven, so let them air dry for two days before painting.

Paint the handles with craft paint and personalize them with the campers' names. After the paint dries, seal with a clear coat of acrylic spray to make the roasters last a lifetime. Not including drying time, eight roasters will take about two hours to make (an hour to form the handles, 45 minutes to paint, and 15 minutes to clear coat). What a cool campout keepsake! (Pop a cork on the end for safety.)

FUN FAN FAVORS

Look online for handheld, programmable, light up, LED message fans. Kids love these battery-operated gizmos. You can program a personal message that lights up when the fan blades spin. (Note: Some manufacturers require large minimum quantities. Keep looking and you'll find them by the dozen.)

CAMPOUT DECORATIONS

PITCH A HOMEMADE TENT

Tie a length of rope tightly between two trees about four feet off the ground. Drape a large sheet or tarp over the rope and stake down the four corners. Use large trash bags or a tarp under the sleeping bags to keep them from getting damp. (Keep in mind, this type of tent will not keep the bugs or critters out, so make sure your campers are the adventurous type before you decide which to use.)

COOL IDEA!

Even if you decide that the campers need to sleep inside the house, build a homemade tent outside for the kids to hang out in before it's time to go to sleep.

PITCH A STORE-BOUGHT TENT

If you don't already have one, borrow one from a neighbor or a friend. Your local supercenter will also have a good selection of inexpensive tents that are easy to assemble. A four-person tent can easily sleep six kids. As with any tent, make sure to locate it on flat ground, and at least 20 feet from the campfire.

LIGHTS

Hang twinkling holiday lights around the perimeter of camp. They'll cast a soft glow on the party, and scare away any monsters that may be lurking!

BUILD A CAMPFIRE- THE REAL DEAL

You'll need a shovel and a husband (or a teenage helper). Check local ordinances to make sure backyard fires are permitted; then, choose a flat, dry location at least 50 feet from any structure. It should have a clear view of the sky, not be obstructed by tree branches. Use a rake to remove leaves and debris. Create a 3-foot diameter hole that is 12" deep. Place stones around the hole, partially in the ground. Pack soil around the stones. Gather kindling to start the fire and larger logs to maintain the fire. Stack the kindling in a teepee. Crumple newspaper and place under the teepee structure. Light the paper and gently fan the flames. Continue adding kindling and larger logs as the fire becomes stronger.

BUILD A CAMPFIRE- THE GENERAL IDEA

If you don't have the desire or ability to dig your own campfire, a store-bought fire pit will work just fine. These shallow metal bowls usually sit off the ground in a small frame. You can purchase one at your local supercenter. As with the real campfire, make sure the area is flat and clear of leaves and debris. Pre-cut firewood works best in fire pits because it is already a usable size.

ABOUT CAMPFIRES:

- Don't use gasoline or lighter fluid to start the fire. Paper works just dandy!
- Don't use store-bought fire starter logs to cook or roast marshmallows. The chemicals will transfer to your food.
- Always make sure embers are cool before you leave the area.
- Always keep a working garden hose nearby.
- And most importantly, never leave children unattended near a fire!

PAINTED SIGNS

Use black craft paint, a 1-inch paintbrush, and pieces of cardboard to make fun signs to hang around camp:

- Don't Feed the Bears!
- No Hunting!
- Caution! Falling Rocks!
- Cut out a Latrine directional arrow
- Paint a giant Camp "Pacino" sign, and hang it over your front porch.
- Use glow-in-the-dark paint to make eyes. Attach them to trees and deck posts.

TABLE COVERS

Pick up a checkered vinyl tablecloth at your local supercenter for a few dollars. It'll be easy to wipe clean, and stay in place overnight with a few pieces of duct tape. Cut placemats out of brown paper bags. Give the campers a bucket of crayons to decorate their own placemats.

EXTRA SUPPLIES TO CONSIDER...

Bug zapper or bug spray, oven mitts, fire poker, batteries, lawn chairs, 5-gallon buckets or plain old logs to sit on.

CAMPOUT EVENING EATS

TRAIL MIX PARTY STARTERS

In a large bowl, mix raisins, pretzels, peanuts, M&M's, Cheerios/Chex and chocolate chips. Pour a few inches of the mix into brown, paper lunch bags. Write each camper's name on a bag with permanent marker.

COOL IDEA!

Line up the bags on the end of the picnic table. As the campers arrive, have the Birthday Kid be in charge of directing guests to where they can put down their sleeping bags and belongings, and then to find their snack bags. This will give you time to chat with, and reassure any nervous parents.

SNACK BUFFET

Line up several clear plastic canisters with lids on a picnic table. Fill them with jerky sticks, pretzel rods, licorice vines; fruit roll ups, peanuts in the shell, sunflower and pumpkin seeds.

WATERMELON SLICES

Slice into wedges or cubes, and make sure the campers save the seeds for the spitting contest!

ANTS ON A LOG

Cut celery stalks into 4-inch pieces. Fill the celery *logs* with cream cheese spread or peanut butter and top with raisin *ants*.

VEGGIE CUPS

Easy Peasy! Line up a row of Dixie cups on the counter. Pour one-half inch of Ranch salad dressing into each cup. Fill the cups with carrot sticks, celery sticks, and pretzel sticks.

CORN ON THE COB

Place pieces of corn on the cob on individual sheets of aluminum foil. Add butter and salt and top with two ice cubes. Fold foil and secure tightly. Cook on hot coals or BBQ pit for about 15 minutes. Turn and rotate often. Don't forget the cob holders!

HOMEMADE FRUIT ROLL UPS

Preheat oven to 150. Coat a cookie sheet with non-stick spray. In a bowl, mix 2 cups of plain applesauce, 1 T honey, and 1 tsp cinnamon. Spread a thin layer of the mixture on the cookie sheet. Bake for 6-8 hours until dried. Cut into slices. Try using some of the new flavored applesauces like strawberry, banana, or mixed berry. (Leave out the cinnamon during preparation.) Store the snacks on waxed paper in an airtight container.

PIGS IN A BLANKET

A camping classic! Cut hotdogs in half. Open a can of refrigerated crescent rolls, and place one-half of a hotdog at the larger end of each crescent triangle. Add a squeeze of mustard. Roll, place on cookie sheet, and bake as directed.

ROASTED WEENIES

The first step to roasting a weenie is to find the roasting stick. Short sticks will cause the cook to be too close to the fire. Dry, brown sticks will catch fire easily. The perfect roasting stick is 3 to 4 feet long, green, and forked. Prepare the sticks ahead of time by stripping the bark from the last six inches. Now grab a pack of hot dogs, and carefully push them on to the ends of the roasters.

MUD POTATOES

The campers will get a kick out of making these! Make a bucket of thick mud from clean dirt and water. (Don't use potting soil.) Let each of the campers cover a plain whole potato with about one inch of mud. Place the mud potatoes in the hot coals of a campfire for about one hour. Use metal tongs to remove the potatoes. The mud will have hardened. Let cool for a few minutes. Then crack open, and eat with a squeeze of bottled butter and pepper.

HOBO POPCORN

Before the party, cut several 18"x18" pieces of heavy-duty aluminum foil. Place 1 tsp of oil and 1 tsp of un-popped popcorn in the middle of each piece. Bring the corners together and fold to form a pouch, (make sure you leave plenty of room for the popcorn to pop.) When the campfire is hot, secure the top of each pouch around the end of a stick. Hold the pouches over hot coals, not directly in the fire. Shake constantly until all the popcorn has popped. Use a potholder to remove the pouch from the stick. Let cool for two minutes. Add salt and eat the popcorn right out of the pouch! If a pouch is dropped into the fire, try to pull it out as quickly as possible to avoid flying popcorn.

WHAT ABOUT BOB KABOBS

Soak wooden skewers in water for 10-30 minutes. Slice 1 lb of pre-cooked Kielbasa sausage link into one-inch pieces. Open and drain a can of chunk pineapple. Skewer the sausage pieces and pineapple chunks. Grill on the BBQ pit.

OTHER EVENING FOODS TO CONSIDER:

Corn dogs on a stick, tater-tots, bagel pizzas, chicken nuggets, and pizza rolls are all easy to prepare for a backyard campout.

CAMPOUT BREAKFAST

HOMEMADE DONUTS

While the campers are cleaning up their sleeping bags and camp area, pre-heat one inch of vegetable oil in a large skillet. Open a few cans of refrigerated biscuits. Press your thumb into center of each biscuit to form a small hole. Carefully place them in the skillet one inch apart. Fry until golden brown, using tongs to flip. Drain on paper towel and roll in a bowl of cinnamon and sugar.

SCRAMBLED EGG POCKETS

The day before the party, brown a roll of sausage, drain and let cool. Place in a plastic zipper bag and refrigerate until breakfast. In a large bowl, scramble a dozen eggs. Add one cup of finely shredded cheese, and the pre-cooked sausage. Pour mixture into a large skillet and cook until eggs are done. Spoon mixture into pita pockets and serve with Tater Tots.

PIGS IN A SLEEPING BAG

Brown some pre-cooked sausage links in a skillet. Open a can of refrigerated biscuits, and pre-heat oven according to can directions. Press one browned sausage link in the center of each biscuit. Wrap the ends around and pinch closed. Place on cookie sheet and bake as directed. Serve with pancake syrup for dipping.

QUICK BERRY PANCAKES

The morning before the party, dice some strawberries and put them in a plastic bowl. Sprinkle with granulated sugar, cover with plastic and refrigerate for two hours. Mix up a batch of pancake batter. Drain the liquid from the strawberry bowl and fold them into the batter. Make smaller pancakes. (Nine should fit on a standard pancake skillet.) Let the pancakes cool completely, put them in a plastic zipper bag, and refrigerate until the party. About 30 minutes before you serve breakfast, preheat the oven to 300. Spread the pancakes out on a cookie sheet and pop in the oven until warm. Place a few on each plate and sprinkle with powdered sugar.

MACGYVER BREAKFAST

Pick up a variety pack of individual mini-boxes of cereal. Open the boxes, and use scissors to cut off the tops of each plastic bag. Pour milk right into the bag inside the box; Cereal with no bowl!

CAMPOUT DESSERTS

CLASSIC ROASTED MARSHMALLOWS

Grab your roasting stick and skewer a marshmallow on the tip. Hold the marshmallow about one foot from the flames. (Any closer and it will burn or catch fire.) Once the outside starts to turn brown, it's done. Be careful not to fling roasted marshmallows. They are hot and sticky!

APPLE PIE ON A STICK

Push a stick through an apple. Turn the stick over the coals of a campfire. When the apple peel starts to loosen, carefully peel off the skin. Mix cinnamon and sugar in a bowl. Roll your apple around the mixture until evenly coated on all sides. Roast over the fire for a few more minutes and let cool.

BROWNIE S'MORES All the yummy goodness without the mess!

- Brownie mix
- Graham crackers
- Mini-marshmallows
- Chocolate bars

Line a 13x9-inch pan with foil, and coat with non-stick cooking spray. Place graham crackers into the pan, slightly overlapping the pieces. Mix brownie batter according to the box, and pour over the crackers. Bake as directed. Sprinkle with marshmallows and broken chocolate bars. Return the pan to the oven for three to five minutes or until the marshmallows begin to puff. Break more graham crackers into pieces, and press them gently into the marshmallows. Cool and use foil to remove brownies from pan before cutting to serve.

STRAWBERRY SHORTCAKE

If the season is right, pick up a few quarts of strawberries. Clean and remove the stems. Cut the strawberries in half and toss in a large bowl with sugar. Cover and refrigerate until the party. Serve on pre-made, individual shortcakes with whipped cream.

ROASTED BANANA BOATS

Take a banana and peel down one strip of the peel (where the banana curves). Slice out a piece of banana almost all the way down and set it aside. Fill opening with peanut butter. Place chocolate chips on top of peanut butter. Replace the peel and wrap tightly in tin foil. Cook on the BBQ pit for 10 minutes. Let cool for 10 minutes. Eat with spoons. These can be made several hours ahead of time and stored in the refrigerator until you're ready to grill.

CAMPOUT DRINKS

LEMONADE, SPORTS DRINKS OR KOOL-AID

These will serve easily from a sports water cooler, and will allow the campers to help themselves. Use squeeze sports bottles to prevent spills. (Label them with a camper's name.) When the sun goes down, make hot cocoa!

CAMPOUT ACTIVITIES

COOL TIP!
There's a 50/50 chance that the kids will decide to sleep inside, so rent a few camp movies like, *Camp Nowhere, Parent Trap, Babysitter's Club* or *Heavyweights*.

MOSQUITO BITES
Pass out sheets of small, red dot stickers (mosquito bites) as the campers arrive. The object of the game is to get rid of all stickers by the time it gets dark. Secretly place stickers (bites) on the other players when they are not paying attention. If you are caught, you have to wear your own *bite*. If you are *bit* by someone else, you have to keep the sticker on until the end of the game. The first player to get rid of all of their stickers wins!

OBSTACLE COURSE
Use a ball of string to mark an obstacle course through the yard, around trees and between bushes. Add buckets, hoses, hula-hoops, and lawn furniture to the course. Make challenges like: crawling under a lawn chair, jumping over a series of buckets, walking on a curvy hose, skipping backwards ten times, hula-hooping five hulas, hopping on one foot while holding a basketball, etc. Use a stopwatch to time the players as they work their way through the course. The fastest player wins!

SEED SPITTING CONTEST
Have the players form a line, side-by-side. Pass out cups full of sunflower or watermelon seeds. Let the players take turns spitting a seed as far as they can. Use colored golf tees to mark where they land. Then, have a *spit-off* with the top three spitters!

ABC GAME
Play this fun game while the kids are sitting around the campfire. Start with the letter A. The first player starts by saying...*My name is Andrew. I live in Alabama. I sell apples to anteaters!* The next player uses the next letter in the alphabet. *My name is Ben. I live in Boise. I sell bananas to birds!* As the game goes on, the players make up silly word combinations.

SLEEPING BAG RACES
Make sure the ground is not muddy or rocky. Mark a starting line and a finish line 20 feet apart. Have the campers form a line, side-by-side, with their sleeping bags. When you say *go*, the players must step inside their sleeping bags, and hop, walk or jump to the finish line. The players must stay in their sleeping bags at all times. The first player across the finish line wins.

DONUT BOBBING
Tie string through several donuts and hang them from a tree branch or deck post, (just low enough that the players can reach the donut with their mouths). When you say *go*, the players must try to eat the donut without using their hands. Make sure you have your digital or video camera handy. To make it even more challenging, blindfold the players, or substitute the donuts with apples!

I'M GOING ON A NATURE HIKE
Have the campers sit in a circle. The first player says, *I'm going on a nature hike, and I'm going to pack...bug spray*. Then the next player says, *I'm going on a nature hike and I'm going to pack bug spray and ...binoculars*. Repeating the first player's item and adding their own. Play continues around the circle. Any player that forgets an item is out of the game.

CATCH A JAR OF LIGHTNING BUGS

- Flashlights
- Clear plastic jars
- Small coffee filters
- Rubber bands
- Toothpicks
- Pan of warm water

Find a place where lightning bugs hang out. Pass out unlit flashlights to the campers. Tell them to hold their flashlights close to the ground. When they see a flash, wait two seconds, and turn on the flashlight for one second. Continue flashing the light, on for one second, and off for two seconds. This will attract the lightning bugs. When they come closer, tell the campers to gently cup the lightning bugs in their hands, and place them inside their jar. Cover the top with a coffee filter and a rubber band. Poke holes in the filter with a toothpick. Immerse the jars into a pan of warm water. (Be careful not to let any water in the jars.) The rise in temperature will make the lightning bugs blink faster. Just compare it to the ones still flying around. When you're finished observing the fascinating little guys, release them back into air. Don't pull their blinkers off; that's just mean!

FLASHLIGHT TAG

Divide the campers into teams of two players. Hand each player a flashlight, and tell the campers to plan a secret flashlight signal with their partner (one long, one short, one long flash, etc). Separate the pairs, and give them one minute to run to opposite ends of the dark yard. The object of the game is for each pair to find each other as quickly as possible by sending their flashlight signals. No talking or making any noise. The first pair to reunite wins!

SCAVENGER HUNT

Before the party, print a scavenger list on brown cardstock. Divide the campers into teams of two or three players. Hand each team a crayon and a list of things to find or see around the yard. Set a timer. The team that finds the most wins!

Here's a sample list to get you started:

Acorns	Caterpillars	Mud
Animal footprint	Dandelions	Mushrooms
Ants	Dead bugs	Owl
Bees	Flowering tree	Pinecones
Berries	Flowers	Pine needles
Black bird	Fruit tree	Puddle
Blue bird	Grass	Red bird
Broken branches	Heart-shaped leaf	Seeds
Brown bird	Large bird	Small bird
Bushes	Leaves with holes	Worms
Butterflies	Moss	

RED LIGHT GREEN LIGHT

Have the campers form a line. Let the Birthday Kid be the first stoplight, and stand 20 feet away from the other players. The stoplight faces away from the other campers, and shouts signals. When the stoplight says, *green light*, the campers must race toward the stoplight. When the stoplight turns toward the campers and says, *red light*, all the campers must stop. If a camper is caught moving during a red light, they are out! The first camper to touch the stoplight wins and gets to be the next stoplight. If all the campers are called out before reaching the stoplight, the stoplight wins!

POPCORN

Add the campers' names to ping-pong balls with a permanent marker. Place the balls in the middle of a large flat bed sheet. Have the campers stand around the outside of the sheet, and grab the edge with two hands. When you say, *go*, the campers must raise, and lower the sheet, trying to get everyone else's ball to bounce off the sheet. The last ball on the sheet wins!

OTHER CLASSIC CAMPING GAMES TO CONSIDER:

Wiffle ball, Frisbee, Nerf football, kickball, Badminton, and volleyball are all easy games to play in the backyard.

CAMPOUT CRAFTS

COFFEE CAN CLOGS

Have your friends and family collect metal coffee cans until you have two for each camper. Use a screwdriver or metal awl to poke a hole on either side of the can near the bottom. Let the campers feed a length of narrow rope into the holes and tie knots on the inside of each can. Have each camper stand on the bottom of the cans and hold the ropes tightly with their hands as they clomp around the yard. No running!

GOD'S EYES

Pick up several skeins of yarn and have the campers hunt for two straight sticks about 12 inches long. Demonstrate how to tie the yarn around the middle of the two crossed sticks. Start wrapping the yarn in one direction. At each stick, wrap the yarn around once and continue the next stick. Change yarn colors after every three or so layers. Finish by tying the yarn in a knot around one stick.

PINECONE BIRD FEEDERS

Gather or buy medium-size pine cones. Tie a piece of yarn to the top of each one. Have the campers smear plain-label peanut butter into the grooves of their pine cones (plastic gloves will control the mess), and then roll them in a pan of bird seed. Make sure the peanut butter is completely covered with seed. Send the pine cones home in plain brown lunch bags.

OLD-FASHION LEAF RUBBINGS

Set out a bucket of crayons and a tablet of plain paper. Show the campers where to collect different species of leaves. Turn the leaves upside down, so the veins are on top. Cover with a piece of paper, and rub a crayon over the paper so the leaf shape transfers through. Try bark rubbings or rock rubbings.

PET ROCKS

They're back...and still as much fun!

- Smooth palm size rocks
- Sticky glue dots
- Permanent markers
- Googly eyes, pom-poms, etc.

Set out the rocks and decorating supplies on a big table. Have the campers select their rock and stick pebbles, googly eyes, and pom-poms in place with glue dots. Campers can also use fun fur for hair, mustaches, and beards or apply additional features with permanent markers. Use silver paint markers on darker rocks. Make a rock spotted like a cheetah, or striped like a zebra. Make your own Pet Rock beds out of 4-inch tin pails from the dollar store. Stuff them with leftover Easter grass or shredded brown paper grocery bags. Make a blanket out of fabric scraps.

HOMEMADE KAZOOS

- Toilet paper or paper towel rolls
- Crayons and stickers
- 4"x4" squares of waxed paper
- Rubber bands

Have the campers color and decorate a long or short tube with crayons and stickers. Secure a piece of wax paper to one end of the tube using a rubber band. Poke 4-6 small holes in the wax paper using a toothpick. Demonstrate how to talk, sing, hum, or make noises into the uncovered end to make kazoo sounds.

CAMPOUT CAMPFIRE SONGS

Kids love to sing! So teach them a few fun songs while you sit by the fire.

HERE'S THE CLASSICS MOM WILL KNOW:

Old MacDonald

B-I-N-G-O

The Wheels on the Bus

The Ants Go Marching

Row, Row, Row Your Boat

Do Your Ears Hang Low?

HERE'S THE SONGS KIDS LOVE TO KNOW:

BABY BUMBLEBEE

I'm bringing home my baby bumblebee. Won't my mommy be so proud of me?
I'm bringing home my baby bumblebee. Oh, ouch! The bee stung me!
I'm smashing up my baby bumblebee. Won't my mommy be so proud of me?
I'm smashing up my baby bumblebee. Oh, ugh! What a mess for me!
I'm licking up my baby bumblebee. Won't my mommy be so proud of me?
I'm licking up my baby bumblebee. Oh, how sick that bee made me!
I'm puking up my baby bumblebee. Won't my mommy be so proud of me?
I'm puking up my baby bumblebee. Yuck! Another mess for me!
I'm sweeping up my baby bumblebee. Won't my mommy be so proud of me?
I'm sweeping up my baby bumblebee. (Shrug) Well, I won't do that again!

ON TOP OF SPAGHETTI

On top of spaghetti all covered with cheese.
I lost my poor meatball when somebody sneezed.
It rolled off the table, it rolled on the floor,
And then my poor meatball rolled out of the door.
It rolled in the garden and under a bush,
And then my poor meatball was nothing but mush.
The mush was as tasty as tasty could be.
And early next summer it grew to a tree.
The tree was all covered with beautiful moss.
It grew great big meatballs and tomato sauce.
So if you eat spaghetti all covered with cheese,
Hold on to your meatball, and don't ever sneeze!

GREAT GREEN GOBS
Great green gobs of greasy grimy gopher guts!
Mutilated monkey meat, dirty little birdie feet!
French-fried eyeballs swimming in a pool of blood!
Oops, I forgot my spoon! Oops, I forgot my spoon!
Oops, I forgot spoon! We'll use a straw!

THE TONGUE TWISTER SONG
One flea fly flew up the flue; the other flea fly flew down,
One flea fly flew up the flue; the other flea fly flew down,
One flea fly flew up the flue; the other flea fly flew down.
Oh my, how that's peculiar!
While one flea fly flew up the flue, the other flea fly flew down.
One sly snake slid up the slide, the other sly snake slid down.
One big bug bled black blood, the other big bug bled blue.
One red rooster ran up the road, the other red rooster ran down.
One pink porpoise popped up the pole,
The other pink porpoise popped down.

THE SONG THAT NEVER ENDS!
This is the song that never ends. It just goes on and on my friends.
Somebody started singing it not knowing what it was,
And they continued singing it forever just because... (Repeat)

CHICKEN LIPS AND LIZARD HIPS
When I was just a camper, I never liked to eat.
The cook put things on my plate, and I'd dump them on his feet.
But then one day he made this soup, and I ate it all in bed.
I asked him what he'd put in it, and this is what he said,
Oh, chicken lips, and lizard hips, and alligator eyes,
Monkey legs, and buzzard eggs, and salamander thighs,
Rabbit ears, and camel rears, and tasty toenail pies,
Stir them all together. It's called cook's surprise.
I went into the bathroom and stood beside the sink.
I said I'm feeling slightly ill, I think I need a drink.
The cook said I've got just the thing. I'll get it in a wink.
It's full of stuff like protein, and vitamins I think.
Oh, chicken lips, and lizard hips, and alligator eyes,
Monkey legs, and buzzard eggs, and salamander thighs,
Rabbit ears, and camel rears, and tasty toenail pies,
Stir them all together. It's called cook's surprise!

MISS LUCY
(May be inappropriate for younger kids)
Miss Lucy had a steamboat. The steamboat had a bell.
Miss Lucy went to heaven. The steamboat when to-
Hello Operator, Give me number nine.
If you disconnect me, I'll kick you in the-
Behind the refrigerator, there was a piece of glass.
Miss Lucy sat upon it, and cut her little-
Ask me no more questions. I'll tell you no more lies.
Miss Lucy's out in the tree house eating chicken pies!

THREE JOLLY FISHERMEN
(May be inappropriate for younger kids)
There were three jolly fishermen! There were three jolly fishermen!
Fisher, fisher-men, men, men! Fisher, fisher-men, men, men!
There were three jolly fishermen!
The first one's name was Abraham. The first one's name was Abraham.
Abra, Abra, ham, ham, ham! Abra, Abra, ham, ham, ham!
The first one's name was Abraham.
The second one's name was I-saac (etc.)
The third one's name was Ja-cob (etc.)
They all went down to Amster-shh, (etc.)
We mustn't say that naughty-word (etc.)
We're going to say it any-way (etc.)
They all went down to Amster-DAM!

THE ANTS GO MARCHING
The ants go marching one by one. Hoorah! Hoorah!
The ants go marching one by one. Hoorah! Hoorah!
(1) The ants go marching one by one. The little one stops to suck his thumb,
And they all go marching down into the ground, to get out of the rain.
Boom, boom, boom, boom!

(2) The ants go marching two by two. The little one stops to tie his shoe,
(3) The ants go marching three by three. The little one stops to climb a tree,
(4) The ants go marching four by four. The little one stops to shut the door,
(5) The ants go marching five by five. The little one stops to take a dive,
(6) The ants go marching six by six. The little one stops to pick up sticks,
(7) The ants go marching seven by seven. The little one stops to pray to heaven,
(8) The ants go marching eight by eight. The little one stops to roller skate,
(9) The ants go marching nine by nine. The little one stops to check the time,
(10) The ants go marching ten by ten. The little one stops to shout, "THE END!"

CHAPTER 6

THE COMPLETE GUIDE TO A FIESTA

In most Spanish-speaking countries, *fiestas* are large public events that bring together entire communities for parades, music, games, and food. Sounds like a cool party to me!

FIESTA INVITES

HOMEMADE MARACAS

- Large plastic Easter eggs
- Cordless drill
- 1/8-inch drill bit
- ¼-inch red or purple ribbon
- Un-popped popcorn
- Colored electrical tape
- Permanent markers and sticker

Drill a small hole in the end of each egg. Feed a length of ribbon through the hole and tie a knot inside. Fill each egg with a spoonful of un-popped popcorn. Wrap a piece of tape around the seam to seal closed. Decorate the eggs with Mexican stickers, permanent markers, or strips of colored tape. Attach your Invite Tags to the ribbon ends. These also make a great arty craft activity. (See Activities Section)

CACTUS SEEDS

Easy peasy! Stop by your local hardware store or nursery and pick up several inexpensive packets of cactus seeds. Use a stapler to attach the packets to your colorful Invites.

MINI-SOMBREROS

These fun little 6-inch hats can sometimes be found at your local dollar store. If not, there are several versions available online. ¼-inch red ribbon can be used to attach Invite Tags to flocked or knitted mini-sombreros, but you'll need to use a hole-punch to attach Invite Tags to plastic mini-sombreros. Order a few dozen extra plastic mini-sombreros to decorate cupcakes, add to the tops of soda bottles, or serve Spanish rice.

Here's an example of how you might word your Fiesta Invite:

> We've planned a FIESTA for the 20th of May
> To celebrate Jessica's 13th birthday!
> There will be plenty to eat and plenty to do,
> So grab your sombrero and show up at two!
> 7735 Main Street
> R.S.V.P. 555-5555

FIESTA FAVORS

Sombreros, Mexican mustaches, beaded bracelets, cactus tattoos, fiesta bubbles, knitted hacky-sack kick balls, coin purses, jump ropes, paddle balls, fiesta pencils, erasers, glow-in-the-dark bracelets, rubber lizards and funny crooked straws make fun fiesta favors.

REAL CACTUS EGG FAVORS

These miniature greenhouses are available online for less than three dollars each, and kids love them! The little boxes come complete with a mini-greenhouse (clear plastic Easter egg), cacti seeds, and soil. All the kids need to do is add water.

REAL MEXICAN JUMPING BEAN FAVORS

If you're having your party between the months of August and November, you can order small boxes of Mexican Jumping Beans online for less than two dollars each. (Those are the only months the beans are in season.) **"What the heck are they?"** Each small plastic box comes with four or five little beans inside. A tiny moth larvae lives on the inside of each bean. When the larva moves, so does the bean! The larvae eats the interior of the bean to survive, and eventually emerges as a small harmless moth. If you hold the clear bean box near the warmth of a low watt light bulb, the beans jump like crazy! How cool is that?

FIESTA DECORATIONS

SOMBREROS! SOMBREROS! SOMBREROS!

What's a fiesta without the fun hats? Pass them out as favors, hang them from the walls or ceilings as decoration, or lay them on a table and fill the brim with chips.

CHILI PEPPER OR CACTUS LIGHTS

String them around the Party room, around deck poles, or between trees outside.

TISSUE FLOWERS

Directions to make these simple fun flowers can be found in the Activities Section. Stick one behind your ear. String them together and hang them from the ceiling. Scatter them around the buffet. Stick them in a glass milk bottle for a centerpiece.

MEXICAN STREAMER CANOPY

You can transform your Party Room in minutes with the help of a friend, two rolls of masking tape, two stools, and several rolls of paper streamers in six festive colors. **How much will you need of each color?** DOUBLE the length of your Party Room, and then add 15 feet. (Example: If the Party Room is 20 ft long; 20 x 2 = 40 + 15 = 55 ft of each color.) Take the first color of streamers and start in the middle of the room. Imagine the Party Room is a giant clock. Have your friend put their stool at twelve o'clock. Cut a length of streamer that will reach from the center of the room to twelve o'clock, adding three extra feet for the *twist and sag*. Attach and hold one end to the center of the ceiling while your friend twists the streamer and attaches it to the wall. Repeat with your friend moving their stool to three, six, and nine o'clock. Change to the next streamer color and repeat the process; attaching the next color at 12:30, 3:30, 6:30, and 9:30, and so on. Make sure your *twists and sags* are even. When you're finished, (if there's no light fixture) hang your piñata in the center.

TABLE COVERS

Bright Mexican-patterned fabrics are inexpensive and easy to find at any fabric store. Finish the ends with a pair of pinking (zigzag) shears. Top with colorful straw placemats from the local dollar store.

SERAPES

Ask your friends and neighbors to borrow the Mexican ponchos and blankets that they brought back from vacation. (Everyone does!) Hang them on the walls around the room and use them to cover the sofa or snack buffet.

TERRA COTTA POTS

Fill small clean pots with tortilla chips. Place a large pot on its side with chips spilling out onto the snack buffet. Use them as centerpieces on your tables and top each with a large tissue flower.

LA MUSICA!

Download or pick up some traditional Mariachi band music. Place a portable CD player behind the sofa or in the corner. Teach the kids how to Mexican Hat Dance!

FIESTA FOOD

TORTILLA SHAPES

Pre-heat the oven to 400. Use cactus and sombrero cookie cutters to cut shapes from flour tortillas. Stack the tortillas to cut more than one at a time. Arrange the cut tortillas on cookie sheets and brush with olive oil. Bake until the edges begin to brown (about 8 minutes). Sprinkle with salt and serve with salsa.

SLOPPY TACO BOWLS

- 6-inch flour tortillas
- Lean ground beef
- Dark red kidney beans
- One jar of salsa
- Ketchup

The night before the party, brown the beef in large skillet and drain. Drain the can of kidney beans and pour ½ into the skillet. Add equal parts salsa and ketchup to moisten meat. Let the mixture cool, spoon into a plastic zipper bag, and refrigerate until the party. Pre-heat oven to 350, twenty minutes before you're ready to serve. Microwave the tortillas on HIGH for 30 sec. and then press each into a section of large muffin pan. Fold back edges, leaving opening in center of each for filling. Bake 10 minutes. Re-heat the filling mixture in the microwave until warm, and spoon into tortilla bowls. Top with shredded lettuce and cheese, tomatoes and sour cream.

TAQUITOS, MINI-TACOS, OR CHIMICHANGAS

Crisp and heat these frozen snacks in the oven. Serve with sour cream, salsa, and a snack-size Crock-Pot filled with warmed nacho cheese. Easy peasy!

BBQ CHICKEN BURRITOS

Bake several boneless chicken breasts as usual. Let cool and place on a cutting board. Use two forks to shred the chicken into small pieces, and then place into a skillet. Add BBQ sauce to moisten and sprinkle in dark brown sugar. Bring to a simmer. Add two spoonfuls of the filling to each flour tortilla. Top with shredded cheese and roll as usual. Slice diagonally in half and serve.

SOUTH OF THE BORDER POPCORN

- 1/4 cup Parmesan cheese
- 1 T chili powder
- 1 tsp salt
- 1/2 tsp garlic powder
- 1/4 tsp cayenne pepper

Mix in a bowl, and sprinkle over warm, popped popcorn.

FIESTA FRUIT

Skewer alternating pieces of strawberries, grapes, cantaloupe, pineapple chunks, and kiwi fruit on 6-inch skewers or party picks. These can be made ahead of time and refrigerated. Serve with vanilla-flavored yogurt.

FESTIVE VEGGIE TRAY

Add carrot chips, grape tomatoes, celery sticks, and cucumber slices to a serving tray. *Fancy-up* the cucumbers by scraping the tines of a fork length-wise down the sides of each cucumber before slicing. Add a bowl of Mexican Dip (equal parts cream cheese, sour cream, and salsa) to the center. Serve in the brim of a sombrero!

NACHO BAR

So simple! Fill a snack-size Crock-Pot with nacho cheese (Velveeta and one-half jar of medium salsa...OR...a can of Campbell's Nacho Cheese Soup). Use a divided snack tray to serve toppings: salsa, guacamole, diced tomatoes, sour cream, and jalapeños.

SPANISH RICE

- 2 T vegetable oil
- 1 1/2 cup uncooked white rice
- 2 cups chicken broth
- 1 cup of chunky salsa

Heat the oil in a large skillet. Add rice, stirring often. When rice begins to brown, stir in chicken broth and salsa. Reduce heat and simmer 20 minutes. This can be prepared the night before and refrigerated. Microwave before serving in mini-plastic sombreros!

OTHER FUN FOODS TO CONSIDER:

PBJ tortilla rollups, Corn chips, dried banana chips or apricots, jalapeño poppers (for older kids) are quick easy Fiesta snacks.

FIESTA DESSERTS

APPLE ENCHILADAS

- Apple pie filling
- 6-inch flour tortillas
- ½ cup of butter
- ½ cup of sugar
- ½ cup of water
- Cinnamon

Preheat oven to 350. Add two heaping tablespoons of pie filling to the center of several tortillas and sprinkle with cinnamon. Roll up tortillas and place, seam side down, in a glass casserole sprayed with non-stick cooking spray. Add butter, sugar, and water to a saucepan. Bring to a boil. Reduce heat and simmer for three minutes. Pour the mixture over tortillas and sprinkle with cinnamon. Bake for 20 minutes.

UNFRIED ICE CREAM

The night before the party, make eight vanilla ice cream balls and freeze on a waxed paper-lined cookie sheet for about an hour. Mix 1½ cups of crushed, Special K Cinnamon Pecan cereal, 2 T. sugar and ½ tsp of cinnamon in a bowl. Roll ice cream balls in the mixture and refreeze until you're ready to serve. Drizzle with honey.

HOMEMADE CHOROS (DONUTS)

While another adult supervises an activity, pop in the kitchen to whip up a quick batch of Mexican donuts. Pre-heat one inch of vegetable oil in a large skillet, and open a few cans of refrigerated biscuits. Press your thumb into center of each biscuits to form a small hole. Carefully place them in the skillet one inch apart. Fry until golden brown, using tongs to flip over. Drain on paper towel and roll in a bowl of cinnamon and sugar.

MEXICAN FLAG CUPCAKE CONES

- One white cake mix
- 24 regular ice cream cones
- One can of frosting
- Two cupcake pans
- Food coloring

Mix the cake batter according to directions, (but only use the egg whites). Divide the cake batter into thirds, using two additional bowls. Add green food coloring to one and red food coloring to the other. Leave the original bowl white. Place ice cream cones into the muffin pans. Use a spoon to add layers of batter, green white and then red, leaving the top inch for expansion. Bake according to the cake directions. Let cool completely, frost, and add red and green sprinkles to the top.

FRUITY PEBBLE COOKIES

- One yellow cake mix
- 1/2 cup vegetable oil
- 1/4 cup water
- One egg
- 3 cups Fruity Pebbles cereal

Preheat the oven to 350. In a large bowl, combine cake mix, oil, water, and egg. Add cereal and mix with a rubber spatula. Drop spoonfuls of dough on cookie sheets. Bake 11 minutes and cook on a wire rack.

FIESTA DRINKS

SODA POP

Pick up some old-fashioned glass bottles of soda, orange, strawberry, root beer, or cream. Kids seem to be fascinated with drinking out of glass bottles. Ice them down in an aluminum washtub (or 35-gallon plastic storage tote). Tie a Mexican blanket around the bottom of the tub, and top each bottle with plastic, mini-sombreros. (See Invites Section)

WATERMELON AGUA FRESCAS

- 8 cups cubed watermelon (no seeds)
- 1 cup of water
- 1/3 cup sugar
- 1/4 cup fresh limejuice
- 1 liter of club soda

Combine half the watermelon, half the water, and half the sugar in a blender. Blend on *puree*. Pour into a pitcher. Repeat with the remaining watermelon, water, and sugar. Stir in limejuice, and add to the pitcher. Refrigerate until the party. Pour into a punch bowl with club soda. Serve in plastic cups. This recipe works with strawberries, cantaloupe, and honeydew.

FIESTA INDOOR ACTIVITIES

MUSICAL HATS

Place sombreros around the perimeter of a table. Use one less sombrero than there are players. Gather the players around the table. When the music starts, the players walk around the table (not touching the hats though.) until the music stops. When the music stops, the players must each put on a hat. The child without a hat is out. Then remove another hat, and start the music again. No tug of war!

PING PONG HURRICANE

Have the players sit in a circle. Place a stool in the middle of the circle and put a ping-pong ball on top of it. Blindfold the first player. When you say *go*, the player turns around three times, and then tries to blow the ball off the edge of the stool. Set a timer for 30 seconds. Let the other kids cheer and guide the player. (Most of the time, players will lose their sense of direction after they spin around. It's hysterical to watch the player try to blow at a ball that's nowhere nearby!)

SILENT MARACAS

Place two chairs 25 feet apart. Gather the kids. Attach a maraca to the leg of the first player using a shoestring, elastic, or masking tape. The object of the game is to get from one chair to the other, as quickly as possible, without shaking the maracas and making noise. If the maraca makes noise, the player is out.

BUST OPEN A PIÑATA

The night before the party, fill a piñata with wrapped candy and small toys. Toss a rope over a sturdy tree limb, a rafter in your garage, or through a hook attached to your deck. Tie one end to the piñata. During the party, have your teenage helper hold the other end to control the height of the piñata. Let the Birthday Kid go first. Have the other kids stand back with their empty favor bags or buckets in hand. (Use masking tape to make a line for them to stand behind and away from the swinging stick.) Blindfold the Birthday Kid. Hand them a stick or broom handle. Spin them around three times, and point them in the direction of the piñata. Let every kid have three swings. Increase the difficulty by raising or lowering the piñata as they swing. Try to make sure each child gets a turn before allowing the piñata to be broken open. Keep a sharp knife to weaken the seams if the piñata is difficult to break.

BEAN AND SPOON RELAY

Divide the players into teams of two. For each team, place a bowl of dried beans at one end of the room, and an empty bowl at the other end of the room. Hand each player a plastic spoon. The object of the game is for the first player on each team to scoop up a spoonful of beans, walk half way across the room to their waiting partner, and transfer their spoonful of beans onto their partner's spoon without touching the beans. The second player has to carry the beans, and dump them into the empty bowl. Any dropped beans have to be put back into the original bowl. The first team to move all of their beans wins.

MEXICAN DUCK POND

- Several dozen Fiesta rubber duckies
- Small wading pool (outside) or aluminum tub (inside)
- Small, *poco* prizes (fiesta pencils, mini-bubbles, candy)
- Large, *grande* prizes (stuffed cactus, sombreros)
- Permanent marker

Fill the pool with water. (If you're in a pinch, use your bathtub.) Mark the bottom of each duck with a permanent marker. If you have three large prizes, write the word *grande* on the bottom of only three ducks. Write *poco*, on the bottom of the rest of the ducks. Toss the ducks into the pool. (If the ducks tip over, squeeze them so they absorb some water.) Let the players take turns choosing a duck and claiming a prize. Continue playing until you're out of large prizes. (Don't throw the *grande* ducks back into the pond once they've been chosen or you'll run out of large prizes.) For younger kids, make sure everyone gets a *grande* prize. For older kids, leave most of the ducks unmarked.

EARTHQUAKE PING PONG

Use colored tape to mark a net across the center of a flat sheet. Have three or four players hold the sheet tightly on each end. Drop a ping-pong ball in the center. The object is for the players to raise and lower the sheet until the ball falls off the opposing team's side of the *table*.

DING DONG SPANISH

Before the party, use index cards to label things around the Party Room with their Spanish name. During the party, tell the kids to try to memorize the words. Near the end of the party, remove the cards, and have the players sit in a circle. Hand each child a bell. One by one, say the English word for an item. Whoever knows the Spanish word rings their bell. The first bell gets to answer.

Here's a list to get you started:

Chair- silla

Table- mesa

Lamp- lampara

Bathroom- bana

Cup- taza

Plate- Plato

Balloon- globo

Flowers- Flores

Hat- sombrero

Present- regalo

Music- la musica

Red- Rojo

Orange- Naranja

Yellow- Amarillo

Green- verde

Blue- azul

Purple- morado

Mustache- mustachos

Cake- torta

Birthday- cumpleaños

Ice cream- el helado

Chips- fritas

FIESTA OUTDOOR ACTIVITIES

RATTLESNAKE JUMP ROPE
Tie a maraca to either end of a 12-foot rope. Have two kids hold the ends, and whisk it back and forth along the ground. The players have to jump over the rattling *snake* without being *bit*. For older kids, raise the rope off the ground several inches. See who can jump the longest without being *bitten*.

POK-A-TOT!
The Mayan Indian civilization lived in southern Mexico from 300-900AD. They had a rich and vibrant culture that included games played to honor their gods; one game was called *Pok-a-tok*, a combination of soccer, basketball, and kick ball. To play a modern version, attach two hula-hoops, about one foot off the ground at opposite ends of a playing field. (Hang on trees, deck posts or the garage wall with rope or duct tape.) Divide the players into two teams, and play with a soccer ball or kickball. The object is to hit the ball in the center of the opposing teams hoop using your arms, hips, shoulders, head, and feet. You cannot pick up the ball or use your hands.

DONUT FISHERMEN
Make two fishing poles by tying string to the end of two broom handles. Have two players stand back-to-back, holding their fishing rods in their hands. Attach a choros (donut) or another easy to eat treat to the end of each string. The players hold their rods straight up and over their shoulder so the treat dangles close to the other player's mouth. The object of the game is to eat the treat from the other player's fishing rod without moving your feet.

MEXICAN KICKBALL

This is a traditional game played in Mexican villages. Divide the players into as many teams as you have kick balls. (Teams of four players work best). The object of the game is for each team member to kick a ball around an obstacle course and the first team to finish the course wins. Make the obstacle course out of buckets, lawn chairs, safety cones, hula-hoops, coolers, etc.

FIESTA CRAFTS

MEXICAN TISSUE FLOWERS

- 6" x 6" colored tissue
- Pipe cleaners
- Scissors

Stack four pieces of tissue paper. Accordion-fold the stack, using approximately one-inch folds to create a 1" x 6" strip. Cut both ends of the tissue strip to round the corners. Pinch the center of the tissue strip. Fold the pipe cleaner over the pinched part of the tissue strip, and secure by twisting the ends together tightly. Fan-open both sides of the tissue paper. Gently pull up each of the four layers of tissue to form the flower's petals. The pipe cleaner forms the stem. Make larger flowers with 12" x 12" tissue.

OJO DE DIOS (God's Eye)

These are yarn and stick creations traditionally made by Mexican Indians. The shape of the cross symbolizes the four elements: earth, air, fire, and water.

- 12-inch wooden dowels
- Various colors of yarn

Tie the yarn around the middle of two dowels to form a cross. Start wrapping the yarn in one direction. At each dowel, wrap the yarn around once and continue the next dowel. Change yarn colors after every three or so layers. Finish by tying the yarn in a knot around one dowel.

PIE PLATE SUN CATCHERS

- Aluminum pie tins
- Bath towels
- Push pins
- Printed shapes
- String or twine

Search the Internet for free printable Mexican or Mayan coloring pages. Look for simple shapes like sombreros, cacti, Mexican suns, and Mayan designs, or find the Mayan alphabet and print the first letter of each child's name! Cut the printed shapes into circles that will fit in the center of the pie tins. During the party, give each child a folded bath towel to use as a cushion when poking holes. Let the kids choose a design to masking tape to the middle. Demonstrate how to punch holes, through the paper and the aluminum, every ½ inch along the outline of the design with pushpins. Remove the paper and add a length of string at the top of each plate for hanging. Use caution with the sharp pins, and check the tins for sharp edges around the holes.

MARACAS

- 1/8-inch ribbon (red, orange, yellow, green, blue, and purple)
- Large plastic Easter eggs
- Un-popped popcorn
- Colored electrical tape
- Cordless drill
- 1/8-inch drill bit
- Toothpicks

Before the party, use a drill to make a ¼-inch hole in the end of each egg, and cut the ribbon into 12-inch lengths. Have the kids choose eight pieces of ribbon in different colors. Hold the ends together and tie into one knot. Use a toothpick to feed the other ends of the ribbon through the hole. (So the knot is on the inside.) Fill each with a spoonful of un-popped popcorn. Wrap a piece of clear tape around the seam to seal closed. Decorate the eggs with Mexican stickers, permanent markers, or strips of colored electrical tape.

MEXICAN WORRY DOLLS

In Latin American countries, children make these tiny people and place them under their pillows at night. They believe that they take away their worries and help them sleep peacefully. These are great for girls or boys (Worry Buddies)!

- Old clothespins (without springs)
- Yarn, felt and/or fabric
- Scissors
- Glue
- Markers

Place all the supplies in the middle of the table and give each kid a clothespin. Demonstrate how to wrap yarn around each leg of the clothespin to make pants, or around both legs to make a skirt. Use a different color to wrap around the top for a shirt. Use markers to make faces. Use markers or yarn to make hair.

INSIDE-OUT PIÑATAS

Gather the kids around a table. Set out several scotch tape dispensers (the hands-free, or wrist dispenser kind are easiest). Give each kid an inflated balloon. Dump a bag of wrapped candy on the table, and let them tape their favorite candy all over their balloons. Kids actually love doing this!

PAPER QUILLING

- White cardstock
- Colored paper
- Paper shredder
- Glue sticks
- Markers

Cut the cardstock into four even pieces. Run the colored paper length-wise through the shredder to make long strips. (You can also buy pre-cut quilling paper at the craft store.) During the party, demonstrate how to roll the strips into small coils using your fingers. (Practice before the party.) Use glue sticks on the cardstock to attach the coils. A yellow coil surrounded by red coils makes a flower. Pinch the coils in half to make pointed oval leaves, fish bodies, or eyes. Pinch them in triangles to make sunrays, fish fins, or hats. Use markers to add stems and details to the cardstock.

CHAPTER 7

THE COMPLETE GUIDE TO A MAD SCIENCE PARTY!

Who isn't fascinated with the mysteries of a Science Lab? All the bubbling potions and creepy things floating in jars; there's a *Mad Scientist* lurking in all of us!

PLANNING A MAD SCIENCE PARTY WILL TAKE A LITTLE MORE IMAGINATION...

Many of the supplies won't be available at your supercenter, but they are easy to find, if you know where to look. Make your shopping list, then check:

- Medical supply companies for surgical masks and gloves
- Laboratory supply for starter microscopes and beakers
- Bartender supply for test tubes (they sell them as shot glasses)

If you can't find what you want locally, you will find it online, often for a lot less.

EXECUTING A MAD SCIENCE PARTY WILL TAKE A LOT MORE PREPARATION...

Things don't always go as planned, so be sure to read through each experiment thoroughly, and practice at least once before the party.

MAD SCIENCE INVITES

MAGNIFYING GLASSES

Print your Invite Tags in tiny print on cardstock. Cut them out, and use ¼-inch black satin ribbon to attach your Invite Tags to dollar store magnifying glasses. Guests will have to use their magnifying glass to read the message!

INVISIBLE INK

Print part of your Invite (see below) on stickers or paper that can be taped to the top of a Mason jar. Then, use a white crayon to write the time and location of the party on plain index cards (see below). Insert the cards into the jars with the written side facing out. Add the contents of an envelope of blue, green, or purple flavored drink mix to each jar. When your guests add water, the dye in the drink mix will reveal the secret! To make it more challenging, write the secret message backwards so your guests have to read it in a mirror!

On the sticker on top of the jar:

> CREEPY EXPERIMENTS AND BUBBLING GOO!
> WE'RE PLANNING A SURPRISE FOR OUR MAD SCIENTIST, DREW!
> ADD WATER TO THIS SECRET COMPOUND
> TO REVEAL YOUR INSTRUCTIONS

In white crayon on an index card:

> NOON MARCH 8 — DON'T DARE ARRIVE LATE!
> 7735 MAIN STREET — RSVP 555-5555

SLIMY TEST TUBES

Easy peasy! Fill plastic test tubes with slippery slime (green gelatin), and secure the caps with narrow strips of packing tape. Add toxic waste stickers and attach Invite Tags with string.

MAD SCIENCE FAVORS

Glow-in-the-dark necklaces, Pop Rocks, Nerds, Lemonheads, plastic safety goggles, Silly Putty, pocket protectors, mini-calculators, black light pens, plastic beakers, and test tubes make great Mad Science Favors!

HOMEMADE LAB COAT FAVORS

Pick up a few packages of men's white pocket t-shirts. Use scissors to cut them down the middle of the front, so they go on like lab coats. Use a permanent marker to write a scientist name for each kid on the pocket, *Professor Pete, Dr. David*, etc.

COOL IDEA!

When the kids arrive, hand each of them: a paper surgical mask, exam gloves, and a pair of hospital booties. Help them tie the masks around their necks to wear during the party. If you can't find them at the dollar store, check the local pharmacy or supercenter.

MAD SCIENCE DECORATIONS

MAD SCIENCE GIZMOS

Add a strobe machine, lava lamps, a fog machine, wave machines, and/or static globes to the Party Room. Check your attic, neighbor's basement, garage sales, and thrift stores for these nifty gadgets. If you can't find them, check a few online auction sites. You can always re-list them for sale after the party.

PLASTIC BEAKERS

Fill beakers or clear canisters with water and food coloring. Add plastic eyeballs, rubber frogs, worms, and bugs. Place the beakers around the Party Room and on the buffet table.

BLACKLIGHTS. BLACKLIGHTS. BLACKLIGHTS!

There isn't an easier way to transform your Party Room than to switch out your regular light bulbs for blacklights. Under a true blacklight, white and light colored fabrics will glow, and neon colors will dazzle. Cover any windows with black construction paper, or black trash bags to enhance the effect. These bulbs can be found at your local hardware store for a few dollars each.

NOTE:

Make sure that the blacklight bulbs you buy are the compact florescent (squiggly tube) bulbs, and NOT incandescent (regular shaped) bulbs. Regardless of what the package says, regular-shaped blacklight bulbs give off a purple light, and do not make things glow beyond a few inches. A 13-watt compact florescent (CF) blacklight bulb will fit any standard incandescent socket and has a glow range of 6-8 ft.

SURGICAL GLOVES

Skip the balloons. Inflate white and blue latex gloves with helium, or inflate them with regular air, and tie along a length of string to hang across the Party Room.

CHALKBOARD

Set up an easel near the entrance to the Party Room. Use chalk to make a list of your planned activities. Write them like mathematical equations. (Mentos + tonic water + black light = X)

MICROSCOPES

If you can find inexpensive starter microscopes, line them up in a row on a table. Use prepared slides or make your own with plant leaves, carpet fiber, dog hair, and onionskin. Be the coolest-mom-on-the-entire-planet, and hand them out as party favors!

TABLE COVERS

Cover the tables with plain white fabric, or find chemistry symbol printed material at the fabric store. Make table runners and placements out of bubble wrap.

HAZARD SIGNS

Print a biohazard sign for your refrigerator door. Add radiation warnings to your television and microwave. Hang a toxic waste sign on your bathroom door. There are tons of scientific symbols available online.

DRY ICE -- THE PROS

- Dry ice can transform the atmosphere of any party!
- It evaporates into a cool, low-sinking fog when placed in water.
- At *adult* parties, it can be added to punch bowls to make bubbling brew.
- Many cool science experiments involve dry ice. (See Activities Section)

DRY ICE -- THE CONS

- *Dry ice will burn exposed skin on contact!*
- You must *always* wear gloves and use tongs when handling dry ice.
- You must *never* store it in airtight containers or unventilated rooms.
- Most importantly, *never* use dry ice in children's punch!

So, if your guests are old enough to truly understand the danger of dry ice, then by all means, make it part of your party. Use discretion, and consult your local ice manufacturer for more tips for safely handling dry ice. If you want to make **DRY ICE FOG**, place it out of reach, in a bowl or beaker with a few inches of water. When the water dips below 40 degrees, the fog will stop.

MAD SCIENCE FOOD

THE SNACK LAB
Line up several matching glass fishbowls, and fill them with grapes, carrots, Nerds, Warheads, Lemon Drops, Airheads, Pixie Stix, Pop Rocks, and gummy creatures.

MELON MOLECULES
Use the melon-baller to make balls of cantaloupe, watermelon and honey dew. Connect three balls together using toothpicks to form a triangle. Stack triangles of all three colors top of each other in a clear plastic cup to resemble molecules.

POPCORN GEYSER
Set a Popcorn Air Popper in the middle of a table. Gather the kids around the table and hand each of them a plastic bowl. Pour the un-popped corn into the top, and leave the lid off. (Keep hands away from hot popper!) Wait a few minutes and catch the popcorn as it flies out.

GRAVITY-DEFYING BACON AND MAC BOWLS
The morning of the party, pre-heat the oven to 400. Open two, one-pound packages of thick-sliced, quality bacon. (The cheap stuff has too much fat.) Turn a large muffin pan upside-down. (Yes, upside-down!) Cut a slice of bacon in half, and form a T-shape over each of the inverted cups. Wrap two slices of bacon around each cup, weaving in and out of the T-shaped pieces. Spiral another strip around the outside of the bacon *basket* on each cup. Place in the oven. Add a deep cookie sheet on the rack below to catch all the drippings. (There will be a lot!) Bake 45 minutes or until the bowls are crispy and brown. Let cool and invert onto a paper towel until you're ready to serve. Prepare a regular box of macaroni and cheese as directed, and spoon into the bacon bowls to serve.

OSMOSIS CELERY
Add celery stalks to glasses of water tinted with food coloring. After the stalks have absorbed the color, slice them into pieces. Arrange them in a shallow bowl of ranch dip or peanut butter.

MOLD SPORE BURGERS
Mix green food coloring with ground turkey. (Hamburger doesn't work.) Form into small patties. Grill or fry as usual. Serve on dollar rolls with shredded lettuce, shredded cheese, and a side of tater tots.

RADIOACTIVE WRAPS
In a small bowl, mix dry ranch salad dressing into a brick of cream cheese with a fork. Spread a thin layer of the cream cheese mixture on a spinach tortilla. Add slices of the turkey and cheese, and shredded lettuce. Roll the tortilla (tucking in the ends), wrap in wax paper, and cut diagonally in half. Seal with a radiation-warning sticker, and serve with shoestring potato sticks.

MAD SCIENCE DESSERTS

BRAINY CUPCAKES
Bake yellow or cherry-chip cupcakes as directed on the package. Let cool. Mix white frosting in a bowl with red food coloring until the frosting is a *brainy* pink color. Spoon the frosting into a plastic zipper bag. Snip off the corner of the bag to make a hole the size of a pea. Squeeze out frosting in *S* shapes across each cupcake to make them look like little brains!

FROZEN SODA POPS
Easy peasy! Fill a plastic pop-sicle tray with strawberry, orange or grape soda. Allow room for expansion. Cover tightly with clear plastic wrap. Add pop-sicle sticks and freeze. If you don't have a pop-sicle tray, use an ice tray and toothpicks.

CRAZY CRISPY TREATS

- 8 cups crispy rice cereal
- 8 cups mini-marshmallows
- ½ stick butter
- ½ envelope of green drink mix
- ½ envelope of blue drink mix

Spray two 8x8-glass casserole dishes with cooking spray. Melt the butter in a large pot. Add marshmallows and stir until melted. Remove one-half of the marshmallow mixture into a separate bowl and add one-half envelope of green drink mix into the pot. Add one-half envelope of blue drink mix into the separate bowl. Add 4 cups crispy rice cereal to each mixture, and use a rubber spatula to coat the cereal evenly in each. Use waxed paper to press each mixture into a glass casserole. Let cool and cut each into squares. Remove squares from each casserole and serve together on a serving dish. If you make these the night before the party, be sure to store them in an airtight container.

MAD SCIENCE ICE CREAM

- Whole milk
- Vanilla
- Sugar
- Chocolate syrup
- Rock salt
- Duct tape
- Quart-size plastic zipper bags
- Gallon-size plastic zipper bags

Before the party, fill quart-size zipper bags with ½ cup of whole milk, 1 tsp vanilla, 1 T sugar, and a squirt of chocolate syrup. Zip the bags closed and seal with duct tape. Refrigerate until kids arrive. Hand each one a gallon zipper bag filled halfway with ice and ¼ cup of rock salt. Put a bag of ice cream mix inside each gallon bag. Secure closed with duct tape. Have kids gently shake and roll their bags until the ice cream in the interior bag feels firm. Remove the small bag, wipe dry, and cut off the top. Eat right out of the bag!

GLOW IN THE DARK JELL-O

Prepare a few boxes of any flavor gelatin, substituting tonic water for regular water. Refrigerate until firm. Use cookie cutters to cut out shapes. Shine a black light on the gelatin. No matter what flavor or color you use, the gelatin will glow bright blue under a black light. This is the fluorescence of the Quinine in the tonic water. (Quinine also gives tonic water a distinctive bitter flavor that you might taste in the gelatin. Lessen this bitterness by using half-tonic water and half-tap water.)

MAD SCIENCE DRINKS

TOXIC POTION

In a saucepan, mix 1-1/2 cups of apple juice and lime gelatin. Cook the mixture over low heat until the gelatin dissolves. Remove from heat, and stir in another 1-1/2 cups of apple juice. Refrigerate until thickened. Divide the mixture evenly among six plastic cocktail cups. Slowly pour orange-flavored drink mix down the side of each glass. It will float on top of the gelatin!

FRANKENSTEIN PUNCH

Rinse out and fill two or three surgical gloves with cranberry juice and a handful of Maraschino cherries. Tie closed to prevent leaks. Freeze overnight. As guests arrive, pour orange juice, lemon-lime soda and cranberry juice (2-2-1 ratio) into a punch bowl. Peel the glove off the *ice hands* and float them in the punch bowl.

MAD SCIENCE INDOOR EXPERIMENTS

MY MOM HAS PSYCHIC POWERS!

Before the party, shred and boil ½ head of red cabbage in two inches of water until the liquid changes to dark purple. (Trust me; the smell will be worth it in the end!) Divide the liquid into six clear glasses or beakers. Let the kids guess what color the water will turn as you add different ingredients: Vinegar will turn it red. Bleach will turn it yellow. Baking soda will turn it light green. Dish soap will turn it blue, and lemon-lime soda will turn it light purple!

RAISING RAISINS FROM THE DEAD

Hand each kid a small box of raisins and a bottle of club soda. When everyone is ready, drop the raisins into the bottle, and watch them bounce and come to life!

"What the heck just happened?" The tiny bubbles in the soda are filled with carbon dioxide. When the soda bottle is opened, the carbon dioxide wants to escape, but gets trapped by the wrinkles in the raisins, and causes the raisins to the rise to the surface.

SMOKING SUGAR CUBES

Fasten a 12-inch piece of floral wire around a sugar cube. Apply ash (from burned paper) to one corner of the cube. Hold that corner of the cube in a candle flame until it starts to burn, and then remove it. The cube will drip a sticky black liquid, and at the same time, it will shoot out tiny rings of smoke!

LIFESAVER LIGHTNING

Take all of the kids into the bathroom, and turn off the lights. Stand there for a few minutes until everyone's eyes have a chance to adjust. Gather the kids around the bathroom counter to watch you use pliers to crush Wint-O-green Lifesavers (not sugarless) over a paper plate. The candy will emit tiny sparks, as it's broken! Hand each kid a roll of Wint-O-green Lifesavers, and tell them to watch their mouths in the mirror. When they crush the candy between their teeth, blue and green sparks will pop out of their mouths! (It doesn't hurt!)

"What the heck just happened?" Believe it or not, it was a miniaturized version of lightning! When sugar crystals are crushed, the pieces become charged with electricity. This excites nitrogen molecules in the air and makes them emit light. Pretty cool!

FLOATING ICE CUBES

Place a slightly melted ice cube on a plate. Lay a piece of red cotton thread across the top of the cube. Sprinkle table salt over the thread. Wait ten seconds and pick up the ends of the thread. The ice cube will float below the thread.

"What the heck just happened?" Salt water has a lower melting point than plain water, so adding salt re-froze the water into ice, and captured the thread in the process.

SECRET EGG TRICK

Before the party, boil some eggs. Gather the kids around the kitchen counter. (The table can be bumped too easily.) Hand each kid an egg. Let them try to balance it on one end. After several minutes of frustration, show them the trick. Add a small pile of salt to the counter top. Carefully balance an egg in the pile, and slowly blow away the salt. The weight of the egg will hold a few granules in place, holding the egg upright. The egg hides these granules and makes it look like it is perfectly balanced!

INSTANT COTTAGE CHEESE

Pour two T of vinegar into a glass of whole milk. The milk immediately separates into a mixture of white lumps and clear liquid. If you pour the liquid through a coffee filter, the remaining solids are cottage cheese!

FLOATING WATER

- Clear plastic cocktail cups
- Water
- Index cards (large enough to cover the opening of the cup)

Gather the kids around. Fill a plastic cup halfway with water. Slowly pour it into the sink. Fill the cup again, halfway with water. Now place an index card on the top of the cup, so that it covers the entire top. Press down firmly as you rotate the cup upside down. Hold the card in place for a few seconds, and then slowly remove your hand. The card should stay in place, and the water should float in the cup with nothing holding it up!

"What the heck just happened?" When you poured the water, gravity was pulling it down into the sink. When you added the card, air pressure pushed up on the card, and cancelled out the gravity!

MAGIC MILK

- Whole milk
- Food coloring
- Dish liquid
- Cotton swabs
- Plate

Dip the tip of a cotton swab in dish liquid, and set it aside. Gather the kids around the table. Pour enough milk onto a plate to cover the bottom. Drop food coloring onto the milk. Dip the tip of a plain cotton swab into the center of the milk. Nothing happens. Now, dip the tip of the dish liquid swab into the center of the milk. The colors will start to swirl on their own. The soap sets the milk protein molecules in motion!

CORNSTARCH CAPERS

Kids love this amazing activity. Empty four cups of cornstarch into a bowl, and stir with a wooden spoon while you add up to two cups of water. The mixture needs to be the consistency of thick pancake batter. Let one child slowly stick their hand into the mixture, and slowly pull it out. (It's covered with goo.) Let another child smack the mixture with a flat hand. (The mixture becomes a solid like gelatin.) Now let one child grab a handful of the mixture, and roll it between their palms. As long as they're rolling, a ball will form; when they stop, the ball disappears!

"What the heck just happened?" When you mix cornstarch and water, you make what's called a non-Newtonian liquid; a liquid that acts like a solid under pressure (the slap or ball roll).

COOL TIP!

Quicksand is another non-Newtonian liquid. If you're ever caught in quicksand, slowly work your way out, so the sand doesn't become a solid!

MAGNET MANIA

Fill several plastic cups halfway with water and three paper clips. Hand each kid a magnet. Ask them to try to get the paper clips out of the cup without getting their hands wet. Move a magnet around the outside of a compass to see what happens. Toss a strong magnet (stronger than a refrigerator magnet) into a bowl of crushed, iron-fortified, breakfast cereal. The iron-fortified crumbs will stick to the magnet. Hold a stronger magnet above the weaker magnet and watch the cereal particles jump to the stronger magnet.

HOMEMADE SILLY PUTTY

Mix two cups of white school glue, and one cup of liquid starch. Add a few drops of food coloring. Mix and set aside until dry, and then pull out globs of Silly Putty! Store the putty in plastic Easter eggs.

DIRTY LINCOLNS

- Vinegar
- Salt
- Mason jar
- Dirty pennies

Fill the jar halfway with vinegar, and add a spoonful of salt. Drop several pennies into the jar. Wait five minutes. Take half of the pennies out of the jar, and lay them on a paper towel. Take the other half of the pennies out of the jar, and rinse them with water before laying them on the paper towel. At first, both sets will be shiny from the salt and vinegar cleaning. Wait two minutes. Do the two sets of pennies still look the same? The rinsed set will still be shiny. The non-rinsed set of pennies will start to turn bluish-green!

"What the heck just happened?" The non-rinsed set of pennies still had some of the salt and vinegar solution on them. When that solution was exposed to air, it caused the pennies to oxidize!

FRUIT BATTERIES

- One plastic candle light (The kind that goes in a window at Christmas.)
- Lemon, orange, or grapefruit
- 2-inch zinc nails
- 2-inch copper nails
- Wire stripper

Cut off plug end of the light with wire strippers. Separate the two wires and strip off 3 inches of insulation from each. Set the fruit on a table and roll it around to soften it without breaking the skin. Insert one zinc and one copper nail into the fruit 2 inches apart. (You don't want them touching.) Wrap one wire around the head of the copper nail. Form the other wire into a small loop, big enough to fit over the head of the zinc nail. Connect the second wire to the zinc nail, and the light will turn on!

HOMEMADE FLUBBER

BOWL A - ¾-cup water, 1-cup white glue, and green food coloring

BOWL B - ½-cup water, 2 tsp of Borax laundry powder.

When the kids are around, pour the first bowl into the second bowl. No need to stir, just reach in, and pull out a glob of Flubber!

MAKE A RAINBOW DENSITY COLUMN

In three separate glasses, add green food coloring to water, blue food coloring to vegetable oil, and purple food coloring to rubbing alcohol. Gather the kids around the table and place a tall, clear cylindrical vase in the middle. Slowly pour ½ cup of each of these liquids into the vase (not touching the sides), in the order they are listed below, from most dense to least dense. Density causes the layers to stay in place, and demonstrates how tightly the molecules are packed in each liquid.

1. Honey
2. Pancake syrup
3. Yellow dishwashing liquid
4. Green water
5. Blue vegetable oil
6. Purple rubbing alcohol

HOMEMADE LAVA LAMP

- One 1-liter, empty, clear soda bottle
- 3/4 cup of water
- 1 liter of vegetable oil
- Alka Seltzer tablets
- Food coloring

Pour ¾ cup of water into the empty bottle. Use a funnel to pour the vegetable oil into the bottle until it's almost full. Wait until the oil and water separates, and add ten drops of food coloring. The drops will pass through the oil and mix with the water. Break an Alka Seltzer in half, and drop half of the tablet into the bottle. Watch it sink to the bottom as the lava starts to blob. Add another tablet to keep it going.

HOMEMADE GLUBBER

Mix one tsp of Metamucil, one cup of water, and five drops of red food coloring in a glass cereal bowl. Microwave on high until the mixture starts to bubble. Let cool. Repeat microwaving and cooling four more times. Pour the mixture onto a cookie sheet and let cool. Use a spatula to separate into pieces of rubbery Glubber! Send samples home in plastic zipper bags.

HOMEMADE ORANGE SODA

- One orange
- One glass
- Water
- 1 tsp baking soda
- 1 tsp sugar

Squeeze juice from the orange into your glass. Add an equal amount of water. Stir in a teaspoon of sugar, and a teaspoon of baking soda. Take a sip. It will be fizzy and taste like orange soda! The bubbles are a reaction between the orange juice (acid) and the baking soda (base) that produces carbon dioxide gas, the same stuff that makes store-bought soda fizzy.

HOMEMADE CLOUDS IN A BOTTLE

- Clear, empty 2-liter bottle
- Bicycle tire foot pump
- A cork to fit the bottle top
- Rubbing alcohol
- Water
- Matches

Add 4 teaspoons of water, and 4 teaspoons of rubbing alcohol to the empty bottle. Poke the pump needle all the way through a cork. Light a match and blow it out. Drop the un-lit, smoky match inside the bottle, and place the cork in the top. Hold the cork while you pump enough air for the bottle to get hard (10-12 pumps). When you remove the cork and needle, the sudden low pressure in the bottle creates a real cloud! When you put the cork back in and start adding pressure again, the smoke particles compress, and the cloud disappears. Cool!

MAD SCIENCE OUTDOOR EXPERIMENTS

SODA GEYSERS (DAYTIME)

- One roll of Mentos candies
- One 1-liter bottle of carbonated soda (diet is less sticky)
- Paper or cardboard

The trick to making an awesome geyser is to drop the candies into the bottle all at once. Unwrap the Mentos and stack them in a tube made from stiff paper. Line up the tube with the open bottle of soda. When everyone is ready, release the candies into the bottle, and stand back! (The kids will want to try this awesome activity, over and over, so make sure you buy extra supplies.)

GLOWING SODA GEYSER (AFTER DARK)

- One roll of Mentos candies
- One 1-liter bottle of tonic water
- Paper or cardboard
- A black light

Make sure the tonic water lists Quinine as an ingredient. (That's the stuff that makes it glow.) Remove the label from the bottle. Turn off exterior lights to make it as dark as possible. Place the black light close to the bottle, but still far enough away that it won't get wet. Unwrap the Mentos and stack them in a paper tube. Line up the tube with the open bottle of tonic. When everyone is ready, release the candies into the bottle, and stand back!

ERUPTING VOLCANO

- Wash tub
- Moist sand
- Dixie cups
- Baking soda
- Vinegar
- Red food color

Pour the sand into the washtub. Make a sand volcano with a hole in the center. Place a Dixie cup in the hole. Put in one tablespoon of baking soda and two tablespoons of water in the cup. In a separate cup, add a few drops of red food coloring to two tablespoons of vinegar. When the kids are around, pour the vinegar mix into the center cup. Watch it erupt! You can repeat the activity over and over again.

DRY ICE EXPERIMENTS
(Appropriate for children over age 8)

- Read the Pros and Cons of Dry Ice in the Decorations Section.
- Read through each experiment to prepare everything you need.
- Explain to the kids that dry ice will burn! Use tongs and gloves.

DISAPPEARING ACT

Use tongs to place a quarter-sized piece of dry ice on a plate and a similarly sized piece of regular ice on another plate. Ask the kids what they think the cubes will look like after one hour. Place the plates out of reach, and go perform other dry ice experiments. Come back to check when you're done. The dry ice will evaporate and disappear. The regular ice will melt and leave a puddle!

SMELLS LIKE VENUS

Use tongs to place a piece of dry ice in a pitcher half-filled with water. The dry ice will evaporate and make a cloud of fog. Let the kids scoop the escaping fog into a Dixie cup. Take a sniff. This is what the planet Venus smells like! The atmosphere is composed of carbon dioxide.

SMOKE BUBBLES

Fill a gallon pitcher ¾ of the way with warm water. Add a squirt of dish soap and several drops of food coloring. Mix with a spoon. Use tongs and gloves to place a large (fist-sized) piece of dry ice into the pitcher. As the dry ice begins to evaporate, it will get trapped by the soap, and float out of the pitcher in fog-filled bubbles. Try to catch them in your hands!

SCREAMING LINCOLNS

Use tongs to place a piece of dry ice into a metal bowl. Insert a quarter, dime, nickel, and penny into the jaws of wooden clothespins. Put on a pair of gloves and hold the clothespin close enough, so that the edge of the penny is touching the dry ice. The dry ice will *squeal* as the gas tries to escape against the penny! Try a different coin.

CHAPTER 8

THE COMPLETE GUIDE TO A COOL LUAU!

Before contact with the western world, Hawaiians called their special feasts, 'aha 'aina. They celebrated everything from the launching of a new canoe, to birthdays. Don't you feel smarter, now? Well then, let's celebrate - island style!

LUAU INVITES

REAL COCONUTS

Real coconuts are available at most grocery stores. When you get them home, trim off the excess hair with scissors. Locate the three stem spots and create a funny face with a permanent marker. Tie a length of raffia or twine around each one. Handwrite or print your Invites on parchment paper, cut them apart and roll them up. Attach another piece of raffia through the first piece, around the invite, and into a bow. Make sure you tell your guests to bring their coconuts!

TICKETS PLEASE!

Use your computer to print airline tickets with party details like: destination, departure time, arrival time, and other party information. Staple a silk hibiscus flower to the top corner of each ticket.

SENDING OUT AN SOS

Remove the labels from several water bottles. Add handfuls of sand and seashells to each bottle. Roll up your Invites and place one inside each bottle. Tie pieces of sisal or raffia around the rims.

Here's an example of how you might word your Luau Party Invite:

>**Funny grass skirts and flowery leis**
>**We're planning a LUAU for Gabi's birthday!**
>**October 13th 5 PM**
>**7735 Main Street**
>**R.S.V.P. 555-5555**

LUAU FAVORS

Flower leis, grass skirts, straw hats, sunglasses, seashell whistles, bamboo flutes, glow bracelets and necklaces, flip-flops, hula-hoops, shark-tooth necklaces and sport bottles make great Luau favors. Use an online name converter to personalize the bottles with the Hawaiian name of each guest!

GRASS SKIRT FAVORS

Save some money on grass skirts by purchasing an elasticized grass table skirt instead. Cut sections as big as the children's waists, and use a stapler or thin strips of duct tape to connect the two ends together.

ALOHA LEI FAVORS

As the guests arrive, have the Birthday Kid say, *aloha*, and pass out grass skirts, flower leis, bracelets, headbands, or ankle bracelets. In Hawaii, even the boys wear grass skirts and leis!

LUAU DECORATIONS

WELCOME TO THE JUNGLE

Move all your houseplants into the Party Room. Ask your friends and neighbors to use their silk palms and ferns. (Don't borrow live plants!) Real or fake, add as much greenery as you can. Use a few lighted, inflatable, or jointed cardboard palm trees. There are dozens of varieties available in prices ranging from two to 200 dollars.

FLOWER GARLAND

Pick up or order silk Hawaiian flower garland, and hang it around the Party Room like streamers, weave between the dishes on the snack buffet, or hang from the ceiling fan and light fixtures.

TIKI TORCHES

Even if you're Luau Party is during the day, Tiki torches are an easy way to add tropical charm. Place the torches along your driveway or sidewalk. Use them inside, to accent large potted plants or zip-tie them to columns, poles and banisters. Do I need to remind you *not* to light Tiki torches indoors?

If the Luau is outside, place some Tiki torches around the party perimeter. Use citronella torch fuel to keep the mosquitoes at bay. Torch fuel is very toxic, so keep the torches away from children and food!

MOOD LIGHTING

Inexpensive, white, or island-themed string lights are great to hang around the Party Room. If the Luau is outside, and in the evening, string lights between trees and wrap them around deck poles.

PAINT

Grab some cardboard, and craft paint to make a giant *ALOHA* sign to hang over your front porch. Staple flower leis or raffia to the sign to make it look more festive.

COOL IDEA!

Sketch out a rough design, and pass this project off to the Birthday Kid. You'd be surprised how crafty children can be with a little guidance.

RAFFIA DOOR CURTAINS

Hang a 6-foot raffia curtain over the doorway to the Party Room. If you can't find raffia, seashell and Hawaiian-flower door curtains are easy enough to find online.

FLOATING FLOWERS

The day before your party, stop into your local florist. Ask if they have any broken or ready to discard orchids, hibiscus, or lilies. (Tulips and roses aren't very tropical.) Often, the florist will give them to you for free, or at a significant discount. Keep the flowers refrigerated until one hour before the party. Trim off the stems at the base of the flower. Float individually, or as a group in shallow bowls of water.

REAL COCONUTS & BANANAS

Pick up a *bunch* of these at your local grocery store. Re-use the coconuts for Coconut Bowling, and then crack them open as a party activity. After the party, peel and freeze the bananas to use in fruit smoothies or banana bread.

TABLE COVERS

Bright floral patterned fabrics are inexpensive and easy to find at any fabric store. Finish the ends with zigzag scissors. You can also use grass table skirts to accent the tables. Add bamboo or grass placemats from the dollar store, seashells, and real coconuts. Use colorful beach towels to cover smaller tables and decorate with plastic crab, lobsters, and fish.

SAND, SEASHELLS & CRABS

Crush a few boxes of vanilla wafers to make your own sand, or pick up a bag of real sand at the hardware store. (After the party, have the Birthday Kid clean it up with a shop-vac.) All shapes and sizes of seashells are available at the craft store. If you're near the beach, collect your own, or use the shells you brought home from vacation. Plastic fish, lobsters, and crabs can be bought in bulk online. You will find plenty of ways to use them for the party, and you can always give them as favors!

GIANT SILK PALM LEAVES

Use as decoration around the Party Room, or as doilies on serving platters. You can find these at your local craft store or decorating warehouse. Staple several together to make garland. Use the larger palm leaves as placemats.

COCKTAIL UMBRELLAS

Taste is as important as appearance when serving Hawaiian food. Pop a colorful umbrella into each punch cup and use frilly cocktail picks for serving snacks.

CITRONELLA CANDLES

These do double-duty controlling mosquitoes and casting warm tropical light throughout an evening party. Make sure you keep them away from food and children!

DON'T FORGET THE TROPICAL MUSIC!

LUAU FOOD

ISLAND SNACK BUFFET
Line up several glass fishbowls, and fill them with dried banana chips, grapes, carrot sticks, M&Ms, pretzels, multi-colored goldfish crackers, raisins, peanuts, etc.

FRUIT SKEWERS
Alternate pieces of strawberries, grapes, bananas, pineapple chunks, and kiwi fruit on 6-inch bamboo skewers. These can be made ahead of time and kept refrigerated. Serve with a bowl of vanilla-flavored yogurt.

CHICKEN KABOBS

- 1/4 cup vegetable oil
- 1/3 cup honey
- 1/3 cup soy sauce
- 1/4 tsp pepper
- 8 boneless chicken breasts, cubed
- One can of chunk pineapple
- Bamboo skewers

In a large bowl, whisk together oil, honey, soy sauce, and pepper. Before adding chicken, remove a small amount of marinade to brush onto kabobs while grilling. Pour the mixture into a gallon plastic zipper bag, and add the chicken chunks. Marinate in the refrigerator overnight. The day of the party, soak skewers in water for 20 minutes. Preheat the grill. Drain marinade from the chicken and discard. Skewer the chicken chunks and pineapple. Cook for 12 to 15 minutes, until chicken juices run clear. Turn and brush with reserved marinade frequently.

HAWAIIAN PIZZA

Save some time, and order ham and pineapple pizzas for delivery. Ask the pizza guy to cut the pizzas into squares for easier serving.

PIGS IN A BEACH TOWEL

Cut some hotdogs in half. Open a can of refrigerated crescent rolls. Place one-half of a hotdog at the larger end of each crescent triangle. Add a squeeze of honey mustard. Roll and place on cookie sheet. Bake as directed.

HAWAIIAN TRAIL MIX

Fill plastic coconut cups with a mix of dried pineapple, dried bananas, raisins, shaved coconut, and Cheerios.

ISLAND BAGEL PIZZAS

Arrange plain, sliced bagels on a cookie sheet. Butter the bagels with pizza sauce or BBQ sauce. Add wafer-sliced ham, shredded cheese and a pineapple ring to each. Toast in the oven until the cheese melts and the pineapple begins to brown.

LUAU DESSERTS

VOLCANO CAKE

Prepare a chocolate cake mix according to the box and pour the batter into a greased or non-stick Bundt pan. Bake as directed. In a small bowl, mix powdered sugar and water until it's the consistency of glaze. Add a few drops of red food coloring until it looks like lava. Pour the glaze over the cooled volcano cake.

THERE'S SAND ON MY CUPCAKE!

Make a batch of yellow cake cupcakes according to box directions. Let cool completely and frost with white icing. Crush vanilla wafers into crumbs for sand. Use Fruit Stripe Brand gum in half for a beach towel, and add a cocktail umbrella.

REAL ORANGE SHERBETS

Slice off the top 1/3 of a large naval orange (the kind with thicker peels). Remove the orange flesh from inside with a grapefruit spoon. Refrigerate hollow oranges until needed. Then, add scoops of sherbet ice cream and serve. Remove seeds, puree the leftover orange flesh, and add it to a batch of Fantastic Island Punch.

ISLAND FONDUE

Melt milk-chocolate chocolate chips in a snack-size Crock-Pot or fondue pot. Use skewers to serve cubed pound cake, grapes, strawberries, banana chunks, pineapple spears, apple wedges, pretzels, marshmallows, etc.

FRUITY PEBBLE TREATS

- Fruity Pebble cereal
- Mini-marshmallows
- Butter or margarine

Melt ½ stick of butter and six cups of mini-marshmallows in a large pot. Add marshmallows and stir until melted. Add eight cups of Fruity Pebbles Cereal and mix with a rubber spatula. Pour mixture onto waxed paper and form into a two-inch thick slab. Let cool for 15 minutes. Use a starfish-shaped cookie cutter to cut out shapes and place them on a separate piece of waxed paper. Re-form leftover mixture into another two-inch thick slab and cut out more stars until no mixture remains.

LUAU DRINKS

SMOOTHIES

Gather assorted juices, milk, chocolate syrup, bananas, oranges, strawberries, canned pineapple chunks, and ice. (Don't mix fresh pineapple with milk; it can curdle in your stomach.) Set a blender on the counter and let the kids choose their poison! Serve in tall glasses with colorful straws and wedges of fruit. Popular flavor combos: Pineapple-Banana, Orange freeze, Chocolate-strawberry and Peanut Butter-Banana.

FANTASTIC ISLAND PUNCH

- Orange juice
- Cranberry juice
- Lemon-lime soda
- Oranges
- Maraschino cherries

Slice oranges into ½-inch thick cross-wise sections. Add a drained jar of cherries to the bottom of a small, round plastic chip server. (The kind that has a space in the middle for dip.) Layer orange slices on top of the cherries. Cover with cranberry juice and freeze overnight. As guests arrive, pour orange juice, lemon-lime soda and cranberry juice (2-2-1 ratio) into a punch bowl. Run warm water over the bottom of the ice ring and add it to the punch.

LUAU INDOOR ACTIVITIES

HULA MARATHON

Easy Peasy! Hand each player a hula-hoop. Play some music. See who can hula hoop the longest. The last four players get a second hula-hoop. See who can double hula hoop the longest. The last two players get a third hula-hoop. Whoever triple hula-hoops the longest wins a prize!

OPEN REAL COCONUTS

Use the drain opening of your kitchen sink to hold the coconut while you puncture TWO of the *eyes* with a corkscrew or a ¼-inch bit in a cordless drill. Let the liquid drain down the sink. (It's not coconut milk. It's mostly water. Coconut milk is a processed product.) After draining, wrap the coconut in a towel and place the point of the coconut (where the three eyes are) on a concrete floor or sidewalk. Strike the bottom of the coconut firmly with a hammer. The nut should crack open easily. Bake the pieces on a cookie sheet at 350 for about 15 minutes to make the meat easier to remove from the shell. Eat raw or use a cheese grater to make flakes to toast.

TOURIST TORNADO

Mark two goal lines 25 feet apart. Fill two large suitcases or duffle bags with one of each of the following items:

- Grass skirt
- Hawaiian shirt
- Extra-large flip-flops
- Sunglasses
- Flower lei
- Beach towel
- Beach bag
- Inflated beach ball
- Straw beach hat
- Plastic cocktail cup
- Fancy Straw
- Toy camera w/strap

Place the suitcases on one goal line. Divide the players into two teams. Half of each team lines up behind each goal line. Play some high tempo music. When you say *go*, the first player on each team must put on everything in the suitcase, run to the other goal line with their empty suitcase, take everything off, pack it and zip up the suitcase. As soon as it's zipped, the next player on the team unzips it and gets dressed. The first team to finish wins!

LEARN TO HULA DANCE

Give each kid a grass skirt and flower lei, then pop in the *I Want to Be a Hula Dancer* DVD. This may take some coaxing, but they'll have a blast!

HEADS UP HULA HOOPS

Divide the players into two teams. Have each team stand in line and hold hands. Place a hula-hoop in front of each team. When you say *go*, the first player in each line bends over and picks up the hula-hoop without letting go of their teammate's hand. Each player must pass the hula-hoop over their head and shoulders, step through, and pass it on to the arm of the next player in line while staying connected. If the players become disconnected, they must start all over. The team that finishes first wins!

MALIA RACES

In Hawaii, a racing canoe is called a *malia*. Since we don't have any *koa* trees to make our own *malia*, let's use laundry baskets! Mark two goal lines 20 feet apart with masking tape or string. Divide the players into two teams. Half of each team lines up behind each goal line. Give each team a rectangular plastic laundry basket. The first person on each team sits or kneels in the laundry basket at one line. When you say *go*, the players must push themselves across the carpet to the other line using only their hands as paddles. When the player gets to the line, they jump out of their canoe and tag the next player. The race continues until one of the teams finishes the relay first. For older kids, have them try to paddle backwards.

COCONUT CLEANUP

- Two brooms
- Ball of string
- Several coconuts

Set up an obstacle course with chairs, stools, beach towels, and coolers. Use the string to mark the path through the obstacle course. Divide the players into pairs. Hand the first pair of each team a broom. Place four or five coconuts on the ground in front of them. Set a timer. The object is for the players to work as a team to sweep the coconuts through the obstacle course without losing any. The fastest team wins!

HOMEMADE LIMBO

What's a Luau without limbo? Buy a pre-made limbo set or make your own. It's a lot easier than you think.

- One 8-ft wooden closet rod
- Sand (or Quickset concrete)
- One broomstick handle
- Two empty gallon paint cans
- 3-inch screws
- Smaller drill bit
- Cordless drill
- Measuring tape

Cut the closet rod in half. (Many larger hardware stores will do this for you, if you ask nicely.) Lay the pieces side by side on a flat surface, and mark every three inches from one end. To prevent splitting, pre-drill holes at each mark ¼ of the way in. Change to screwdriver bit and insert 3-inch screws half way into each pole. Insert each pole with the new screws on top into a 1-gallon paint can. Use rocks to keep the bottoms erect while you add sand or concrete. Make sure the poles are equal in height so the limbo notches (screws) are level. Use the broom handle as a limbo stick.

HOW TO LIMBO

Play some upbeat, Hawaiian music. Set the broomstick on the highest notch on each pole. Have the players form a line, and take turns trying to walk underneath the broomstick with their shoulders leaning back, and noses pointing up. They're not allowed to touch the broomstick with any part of their body. After everyone has a turn, lower the broomstick one notch. Anyone who touches or knocks the broomstick down is out. Continue until only one player is able to limbo without knocking down the broomstick.

FLASHLIGHT LIMBO

Clear a floor space and turn off the lights. Have two kids stand a few feet apart, each holding a flashlight. Point the flashlights at each other to create a level beam of light. If the limbo player touches the light, he's out.

ISLAND MEMORY

Before the party, use index cards to write down the Hawaiian word for things around the Party Room. Tape the cards to the items. Tell the kids to try to memorize the words during the party. Near the end, collect all of the cards. Gather the kids in a circle. One by one, say the English word for an item. The first kid that knows the Hawaiian word (or close to it) gets a point. Keep score, and whoever memorizes the most Hawaiian words gets a prize.

Here are some common items found at a Luau Party:

Chair- noho
Table- pakaukau
Flower- pua
Present- makana
Music- mele
Cake- Mea 'ono

Ice cream- haukalima
Palm tree- palama
Volcano- Pele
Coconut- niu
Banana- mai'a
Pineapple- hala-kahiki

LUAU OUTDOOR ACTIVITIES

MUSICAL ISLAND HOP

All you need for this fun game is several plastic dish tubs, (one for each player), music, and bare feet. Set up the tubs in a circle with several feet in between. Fill with water. Have the players stand between the tubs, facing each other's back. When the music starts, the players must hop in a tub, hop out, hop in the next tub, and hop out. When the music stops, whoever is in a tub, (and missed their island) is out. Let the music play a bit longer than you would with Musical Chairs. Since several players will be in tubs when the music stops, the game will go quickly.

CRAB RACES

Use masking tape to mark two goal lines 20 feet apart. Divide the players into two teams. Half of each team lines up behind each goal line. If you can, demonstrate the crab walk (walking on your hands and feet with your belly pointing up). The first player on each team gets into position on one goal line. When you say *go*, the two players crab walk to the other goal line, and tags the next player on their team. The first team to finish the race wins!

THERE'S A HOLE IN MY BUCKET

Exactly what it sounds like! Purchase some plastic beach buckets at the dollar store. Use a half-inch drill bit to make holes in the bottom of each bucket. Test the buckets to make sure the water will leak out in less than 20 seconds. At the party, put two large aluminum tubs (or 35-gallon plastic storage totes), full of water at one goal line. Put two empty mop buckets at the other goal line. Divide the players into two teams. When you say *go*, the first player from each team must use their *hole-y* bucket to scoop water from the washtub, race down to the other goal line and dump the remaining water that hasn't leaked out of their bucket into the empty bucket. The team that fills their mop bucket first wins!

BEACHBALL DODGE BALL

Fill a beachball half way with water. Inflate the rest of the ball with air. (This gives the ball some weight.) Divide the players into two teams. One team makes a circle and the other team stands in the center of the circle. The players on the outside throw the ball at the players in the center. The players in the center run around trying not to be hit. They cannot catch the ball. (That's why it's called DODGE ball!) If a ball hits a player in the head, it does not count. If a ball hits a player anywhere else on the body, that player joins the outside team to throw and catch the ball. The last player in the center wins!

COCONUT BOWLING

Set up empty tin cans or ½-gallon milk jugs as pins. Use real coconuts for the bowling balls. This easy game is fun to play inside or outdoors. Keep score and hand out prizes (or a small trophy) to the best coconut bowler.

SEASHELL HUNTER

Fill a sandbox or giant washtub with dry sand. Bury small seashells in the sand. Set the timer for 20 seconds. When you say *go*, the player has 20 seconds to find the most seashells. Whoever finds the most wins! Add different dry pasta shapes to the sand to make it more challenging.

LUAU CRAFTS

SEASHELL WIND CHIMES

- Pre-drilled seashells from the craft store
- String or yarn
- Pringles can lids

Before the party, use an awl to punch six holes around the perimeter of several plastic Pringles can lids. During the party, hand each kid, one plastic can lid and three 24-inch long pieces of cotton string. Demonstrate how to fold the strings in half (to make six equal length pieces). Tie a knot in the folded end of the strings to make a two-inch loop. Feed each string through a hole in the plastic lid. String shells along the length of each string about two inches apart. Tie a knot after each shell to keep it from slipping down the string. When you've added all of your shells, pick the wind chime up by the loop, and brush the shells with your hand to hear the tinkling.

HAWAIIAN SUNGLASS STRAPS

- Sunglasses
- Elastic string
- Metal crimps
- Pony Beads
- Colorful straws
- Needle-nose pliers

Pick up some colorful, plastic sunglasses at the dollar store, and elastic string and metal crimps (for jewelry making) at the craft store. Cut an 18-inch length of elastic for each kid. Fold one end of the elastic over and use needle-nose pliers to attach a metal crimp, so that there is a 1/4-inch loop that fits snuggly over one arm of a pair of sunglasses. Cut the straws into one-inch pieces. Let the kids thread straws and pony beads onto the elastic, leaving enough at the other end to make another crimped loop. Attach the loops to the arms of the sunglasses.

EASY PEASY SAND ART

- Colored craft sand
- Plastic sand art bottles & corks
- Small funnels
- Several plastic bowls
- Coffee cups
- Spoons
- Beach towels
- Packing tape

Cover the table with beach towels. (Towels are better for capturing spilled sand.) Pour the sand into individual bowls, and place them in the center of the table. Give each kid a coffee cup (to prevent bottles from falling over), a sand art bottle, a funnel, and a spoon. Demonstrate how to hold the bottle and funnel still, while adding spoonfuls of sand. Make colorful layers, and create waves by slightly tipping the bottles. Fill the bottles to the very top. Tap softly to make sure all the sand has settled. Add corks to close. Use narrow strips of clear packing tape to secure corks and prevent spills during the car ride home.

COOL IDEA!

If you don't have sand art bottles, use baby food jars. Make sure the lids are secure before sending them home.

DESIGN YOUR OWN FLIP FLOPS

- Inexpensive flip-flops
- Bright colored yarn
- ½ inch of ribbon
- Tropical silk flowers
- Pony Beads

Wrap long lengths of ribbon or yarn tightly around the straps to cover completely. Tie a secure knot at each end. Use a hot glue gun to attach silk flowers, or add colorful pony beads to the ribbon as you wrap the straps.

TERRA COTTA CRABS

- 3 ¼-inch terra cotta saucers
- 1 ¼-inch terra cotta pots
- ½-inch wooden oval beads
- Red pipe cleaners
- Red craft paint
- Googly eyes
- Hot glue gun
- Paintbrushes

Before the party, fill quart-size plastic zipper bags with supplies. Each should contain 6 red pipe cleaners, 1 paintbrush, 16 oval beads, and 2 tiny pots.

During the party, spread newspaper on the table, and pour the paint into bowls. Pass out one supply bag and two saucers per child. Demonstrate how to paint the bottom and sides of the saucers, the outside of the tiny pots, and the beads. Use paper plates to keep the beads from rolling. Let the pieces dry for 30 minutes. Show the kids how to tie a knot in the end of the six pipe cleaners. Use a hot glue gun to glue the knotted end of a pipe cleaner into each tiny pot. Set the tiny pots right side up and thread two beads onto each pipe cleaner. Thread three beads on each of the remaining four knotted pipe cleaners. Make knots in all six pipe cleaners so that the beads do not slide off. Place one saucer right side up. Lay the exposed pipe cleaner end of each claw at ten and two o'clock. Place two beaded legs on either side at four and five o'clock, and seven and eight o'clock. Add a bead of hot glue around the rim, over the pipe cleaners, and add the other saucer to close, trapping the pipe cleaners between the rims of both saucers. Add googly eyes to the tops.

HAWAIIAN TISSUE FLOWERS

- 6" x 6" colored tissue
- Pipe cleaners
- Scissors

Stack 4 pieces of tissue paper together. Accordion-fold the stack, using approximately one-inch folds to create a 1" x 6" strip. Cut both ends of the tissue strip to round the corners. Pinch the center of the tissue strip. Fold the pipe cleaner over the pinched part of the tissue strip, and secure it by twisting the ends together tightly. Fan open both sides of the tissue paper. Gently pull up each of the four layers of tissue to form the flower's petals. The pipe cleaner forms the stem. Twist the stems together to make leis. Make larger flowers with 12" x 12" tissue.

CHAPTER 9

THE COMPLETE GUIDE TO A PRINCESS PARTY!

A royal life filled with beautiful friends, a dazzling wardrobe, and a handsome prince. Every little girl loves pretending to be a princess!

PRINCESS INVITES

LOST SLIPPERS
What's a Princess Party without a lost slipper? Pick up several pairs of pretend princess shoes at your local dollar store or supercenter. Attach Invite Tags with pink satin ribbon.

COOL IDEA!
After you get the slippers home, use a permanent marker to write the Princesses initials on the bottom of each slipper in the pair. Give one slipper as an Invite, and save the other slipper to use in a Seeking Game. (See Activities Section) Make sure to remind the princesses to bring their lost slipper to the party.

ROYAL INVITES

Pick up several, 6-inch, white, mailing tubes from your local office supply store or post office. Print your Royal Invites in a formal font on parchment paper, two per sheet. Cut them apart, roll, and insert into the tubes. Seal one end closed with a cap or clear packing tape. Pour a spoonful of glitter or metallic confetti into the other end. Seal with another cap. Tie a wide, pink, satin bow around each one before you deliver them. (If you're sending these Royal Invites through the mail, they may require special postage.)

Here's an example of how you might word your Fairy Princess Party Invite:

A splendid party...a majestic cake...

a royal birthday to celebrate!

You are hereby summoned to attend a merry festival

In honor of Princess Jessica!

At noon on the 29th Day of September

Johnson Castle

R.S.V.P. 555-5555

COOL IDEA!

Ask your guests to come to the party dressed as their favorite princess. Pick up a few extra costumes to have on hand. If your party is in November or December, you may be able to find deeply discounted princess and fairy costumes leftover from Halloween. If not, check your local thrift store for dress-up outfits and costume jewelry.

PRINCESS PARTY FAVORS

Anything pink and frilly will do! Look for jewelry, mirrors, candy necklaces, princess stickers, ring pops, hair ties, stick-on earrings, bubbles, lip-gloss, or light-up wands.

FAVOR BAGS

Pink plastic or canvas totes make great favor bags for princesses. The dollar store usually has a great selection of princess and girly favor bags.

PRINCESS DECORATIONS

STREAMER CANOPY

Make the Party Room fit for a Princess in a matter of minutes with the help of a friend, two rolls of masking tape, two stools, and several rolls of paper streamers in THREE different colors. **How much will you need of each color?** Double the length of your Party Room, and add 15 feet. (Example: If the Party Room is 20 ft long; 20 x 2 = 40 + 15 = 55 ft of each color.)

The day before the party, choose one color and start in the middle of the room. Imagine the Party Room is a giant clock. Have your helper put their stool at twelve o'clock. Cut a length of streamer that will reach from the center of the room to twelve o'clock, adding three extra feet for *twist and sag*. Attach and hold one end to the center of the ceiling, while your helper twists the streamer and attaches it to the wall. Repeat with your helper moving their stool to three, six, and nine o'clock. Change to the second color, and attach at one, four, seven, and ten o'clock. Attach the third color at two, five, eight, and eleven o'clock. Make sure your *twists and sags* are even. If you want to use something more royal than paper streamers, use 6-inch tulle or twisted paper ribbon. (See Jungle Safari Party Decorations for details.)

MIRROR, MIRROR!

Use a washable marker to write: "Mirror, Mirror on the wall, who's the prettiest of them all?" at the top of your bathroom mirror.

RIBBONS, BOWS & BEADS

Pick up several 25-yard spools of 6-inch purple or white tulle from your fabric store. (You can order them online for less than two dollars each.) Use the tulle to wrap railings and pillars; make bows for your front porch; swag the fireplace and doorways; make Princess skirts (see Activities Section); or to decorate the Princess banquet table and chairs. Dig through your holiday decorations or check the dollar store for strings of gold or silver beads and crystal garlands. Drape the baubles from your hanging light fixtures or weave them along the buffet table.

SET A ROYAL TABLE

- A week before the party, dig through your dining room cabinets (and those unopened wedding gifts in the attic?) for crystal or silver serving dishes and platters. Ask your mom, neighbors, or friends to use their three-tier servers, crystal punch bowl or silver tea sets. These will turn any buffet table into a royal banquet.
- Cover your tables with shimmering pink or white tulle. Let the fabric hang over the edge, but not all the way to the floor. (Any longer and it will tangle little princess feet.) Where the princesses dine, add white paper doily placemats, and crisp white cardstock place cards, printed with each guest's name, Princess Jessica, Princess Gabriela, Princess Hailey, etc. If you're hand printing the place cards, use a silver or gold paint marker.
- The day before your party, stop into your local florist to see if they have any broken or ready-to-discard, carnations, pink or white roses, and baby's breath. Often the florist will give them to you for free or at a significant discount. Keep the flowers refrigerated until one hour before the party. Trim the stems, and place them in 6-inch single stem vases (from the dollar store) next to the place cards. Scatter the remaining rose petals on the table.
- Use clear plastic plates and champagne flutes to serve drinks and food. (Don't trust little hands with real crystal or china!) Wrap your silverware in white or pink cloth napkins; tie a bow around each, and add to the place settings or display them in a basket.

TRANSFORM YOUR FURNITURE

Use white pillowcases to cover the backs of each party chair. Tie bows around the chairs with wide, pink satin ribbon (wired-ribbon retains its shape the best), 6-inch pink tulle, or narrow strips of fabric. Cover your sofas with white flat sheets or satin fabric. Check the clearance table at your fabric store for remnants. You can use these pieces to temporarily re-cover your throw pillows; Wrap each pillow like a present and secure the back closed with safety pins. Hot pink feather or Marabou boas are also inexpensive and easy to find, and can be used in a number of ways to *princess-up* the Party Room.

PRINCESS FOOD

COOL IDEA!

When it's time to eat, seat the princesses at their table, and let your teenage helper assist in serving treats from silver platters.

PRINCESS TREAT BUFFET

Arrange crystal candy dishes. Fill them with Hershey Kisses, pink taffy pieces, candy necklaces, pastel gummy bears, Pixie Stix, or pastel jellybeans. If you want to serve healthier treats, fill the bowls with fresh strawberries, grapes, melon balls, yogurt-covered raisins, peanut butter-filled pretzels, or Fairy Dust Crunch. (See Recipe Section)

BERRY GRAHAMS

- Strawberry cream cheese
- Graham crackers
- Sliced strawberries

Break the grahams into individual crackers and place them on a silver serving tray. Use an icing bag with a fluted tip to add a fancy dollop of cream cheese to each cracker. Top with sliced strawberries.

PRINCESS PINWHEELS

- Dry ranch dressing mix
- One brick of cream cheese
- ¼ cup of sour cream
- ½ cup of diced ham
- ½ cup of shredded cheese
- Flour tortillas

The night before the party, use a fork to combine the dip mix, cream cheese, and sour cream in a medium bowl. Fold in the ham and cheese mixing thoroughly. Smooth a ¼-inch thick layer of the mixture onto a flour tortilla. Roll tightly, and wrap in clear plastic wrap. Refrigerate until the party. Then use a sharp knife to slice the rolls into ½-inch spirals, and arrange on a party platter.

PINKY SANDWICHES

They're called Pinkie Sandwiches because you have to eat them with your pinkies up in the air! Prepare peanut butter and jelly or turkey and cheese sandwiches as usual. Use a sharp knife to remove crusts and slice diagonally into four triangles. You can also make your tiny sandwiches on 4-inch cocktail white, wheat, or rye bread available in the Deli Dept. When you're finished, slice them diagonally into triangles. Insert a cocktail pick into each wedge.

YOGURT PARFAITS

- Vanilla yogurt
- Granola crunch cereal
- Fresh berries (raspberries, blueberries, strawberries)
- Clear plastic cocktail cups

Arrange clear plastic cocktail cups on a cookie sheet. Add a 2-inch layer of yogurt to each cup, smoothing the surface with the tip of a spoon. Sprinkle on a layer of granola, a layer of fresh berries, and another layer of yogurt. Top off with more berries and refrigerate until the party.

MAGIC WAND PRETZELS

- White chocolate chips
- Red food coloring
- Pretzel rods
- Candy sprinkles

Melt the white chocolate chips in the microwave, stirring frequently. (Be careful not to over-heat. The chocolate will get crumbly.) Stir in a few drops of food coloring until it turns a pretty pink. Hold a pretzel rod over the bowl and use a spoon to drizzle chocolate over two-thirds of the rod, making sure the coating isn't too thick. Roll in a pie plate filled with candy sprinkles, and place on wax paper to let cool completely.

PETITE QUICHES

These dainty little pre-made pastry cups are a perfect princess snack. Check the freezer section of the local grocery or warehouse. Pop them in the oven and serve.

PRINCESS DESSERTS

FAIRY DUST CRUNCH

- 9 cups Rice Chex
- 1 ½ cups of chocolate chips
- ¼ cup of butter
- 1 tsp vanilla
- 1 ½ cups powdered sugar
- 1 box of strawberry gelatin

Add the cereal to large bowl and set aside. Microwave the chocolate chips, butter, and vanilla in an uncovered small bowl. Stir frequently. Pour the warm mixture over the cereal and blend with a rubber spatula. Mix powdered sugar and gelatin in plastic zipper bag. Sprinkle over the cereal mixture. Seal bowl with plastic wrap and shake until well coated.

CHOCOLATE COVERED STRAWBERRIES

I don't know why people don't make these more often. It could not be easier! Gently rinse the strawberries, and let them dry completely on a stack of paper towels. Arrange cupcake liners in a plastic cake server. Use a cereal bowl to microwave a few broken chocolate bars or unwrapped kisses, 30 seconds at a time, stirring frequently until smooth. (Be careful not to over-heat. The chocolate will get crumbly.) Gingerly gather the leaves and stem of each strawberry with the tips of your fingers, and dip them into the warm chocolate. Roll to coat on all sides. Scrape the excess chocolate off on the edge of the bowl and lay the strawberry on its side in a cupcake liner. Cover with waxed paper and refrigerate. These will last in the refrigerator for up to 48 hours before getting mushy.

CHERRY-CHIP ICE CREAM SHORTCAKES

You can make this recipe with just about any combination of flavors. Try vanilla bean ice cream with caramel sauce, strawberry ice cream with strawberry sauce, mint chip or chocolate ice cream with chocolate sauce.

- Twelve ¾-oz. pre-made shortcakes
- ½ gallon cherry chip ice cream
- One jar of chocolate fudge ice cream sauce

Place the ice cream container into your empty sink for 15 minutes to soften. Line up the shortcakes on a clean, dry working surface. When the ice cream is soft (but not drippy), use a metal frosting knife to quickly, fill the shortcakes with ice cream, leveling it even with the rims. Invert one on top of another to form a sandwich. Place on a waxed paper lined cookie sheet and into the freezer for at least two hours. Just before serving, use a serrated knife to slice the hardened sandwiches in half (or quarters for smaller guests). Drizzle fudge sauce over each piece and serve.

CASTLE CUPCAKES

- One cake mix (any flavor)
- One can of white frosting
- Waffle ice cream cones
- Bright pink sugar crystals
- Silver foil cupcake liners

In the foil cupcake liners, bake a batch of cupcakes according to the box directions. Cool the cupcakes and frost as usual. Add a thin coat of frosting to the outside of the waffle cones, and place them upside down on top of the cupcakes. Sprinkle with sugar.

PRINCESS SURPRISE CAKE

- One 10-oz prepared angel food cake
- One box of strawberry gelatin
- One tub of whipped topping
- ¾ cup chopped strawberries
- 1 cup sliced strawberries

Place the angel food cake on a serving plate or glass cake stand. Cut a one-inch-thick horizontal slice from top of cake using a serrated knife. With small knife, cut and remove a one-inch wide and one-inch deep *moat* around the inside center of cake. Place two medium bowls on the counter. In Bowl A, prepare gelatin as directed on box. Remove 1/2 cup of gelatin and pour into Bowl B, and then refrigerate Bowl A for 10 minutes. Add a tub of whipped topping to Bowl B, whisk until blended, and then refrigerate. When Bowl A has thickened, stir in ¾ cups of chopped strawberries, and spoon the mixture into the *moat* of the cake. Replace the top of cake. Remove Bowl B from refrigerator and frost cake with whipped topping gelatin mixture. Garnish the top with sliced strawberries. Refrigerate until serving.

PRINCESS DRINKS

PINK LEMONADE FIZZES

Prepare a few cans of frozen pink lemonade in a large punch bowl. Add a liter of lemon-lime soda. Float fresh cut lemon slices in the bowl.

MAGIC POTION PUNCH
Add ½ gallon of pulp-free orange juice and a 2-liter of strawberry soda to a punch bowl. Serve in plastic champagne glasses with Maraschino cherries.

WICKED WITCH CUBES
Freeze cranberry juice in ice cube trays overnight. Add cubes to a clear cocktail cup filled with lemon-lime soda.

PRINCESS ACTIVITIES

SEEKING LOST SLIPPERS
If you sent Lost Slipper Invites and saved the mate to each, hide them around the Party Room. When the Princesses arrive with their Lost Slipper, tell them that the other slipper is hidden somewhere in the castle. Let them search for their matching slipper to wear during the party. (Make sure you have extra pairs of slippers on hand in case anyone forgets to bring their own.)

ROYAL FASHION SHOW
Dig through your closets, your friends and family's closets, and the local thrift store to find old, fancy, dress up clothes -the tackier the better! Look for things like sequined tops, dresses, (They don't have to be the right size, just sparkly.) old pairs of high heels, flip-flops and handbags that you can spray with gold spray paint. Find some big floppy hats, colorful scarves, sunglasses, chunky necklaces, and bracelets. Put it all in a few laundry baskets and let the princesses go to town dressing up! When they're finished, line them up in another room, and have them show off their creations one by one. Take plenty of pictures while they pose.

FAIRY MAKEOVERS

Set up a Makeover Table and chair (or use the kitchen counter and a stool). Gather sparkling face glitter, lip-gloss, blush, and various ribbons, barrettes or bows. Place a lighted make-up mirror so the princesses can watch their makeover. If you have time and extra help, add braids or banana curls. Use quick-drying, clear glitter nail polish as a finishing touch.

MUSICAL TIARAS

Set up the tiaras around the edge of a table. Put out one less tiara than there are princesses. When the music starts, the princesses walk around the table, not touching the tiaras. When the music stops, the princesses must quickly pick up a tiara to put on. The princess without a tiara is out. Then remove another tiara and start the music again. No tug of war! At the end of the game, give each princess a tiara to wear for the rest of the party.

WHAT'S IN THE PRINCESS' PURSE?

Fill a fancy silver serving tray with twenty Princess necessities: a magic wand, lipstick, hand mirror, necklace, earrings, rings, white gloves, tiara, etc. Gather the princesses in a circle. Set the tray in the center. Give them one minute to look at all of the items. Have them cover their eyes while you remove one item. Let them guess what's missing. Play again, removing a different item, or adding a new item.

PRINCESS SENDS A SECRET MESSAGE

Have the princesses sit in a circle. The first princess whispers something into the ear of the princess next to her. One by one, each princess repeats the whispered secret exactly as she heard it. The last princess to receive the message says it out loud. It is usually completely different from the original secret. You can also play by making goofy faces, but the kids usually collapse into laughter before the goofy face makes it around the circle!

SMARTIE SUCKER

Divide the princesses into pairs. Give each pair a plate filled with candy Smarties, an empty plate, and two straws. When you say *go*, the teams have two minutes to suck the Smarties onto their straw (so that the suction keeps the candy attached to the bottom of the straw), and move them to the empty plate. The team that moves the most wins!

KISS THE FROG

This is a fun variation of hot potato using a stuffed frog. Have the princesses sit in a circle. The frog is passed from player to player while the music plays. When the music stops, the player who has the frog has to kiss the frog! Then move to the center of the circle until someone else kisses the frog, and takes their place in the middle. The last player, who hasn't kissed the frog, wins! Stop the music frequently so the game moves quickly and no one has to sit in the center too long.

HUNT AND SLAY THE DRAGON

The night before the party, fill a dragon piñata with wrapped candy and small jewels. Wrap and tape aluminum foil around a broomhandle to make a sword. Hide the dragon somewhere in the Party Room. The day of the party, let the princesses hunt for the dragon, and then slay him! Toss a rope over a sturdy tree limb or beam, or through a hook attached to your deck. Tie one end to the dragon piñata. Have your teenage helper hold the other end to control the height of the dragon. Let the Birthday Princess go first. (Use masking tape to make a line for the other princesses to stand behind, and away from the swinging sword.) Hand the Princess her sword and let her take three swings at the dragon. Raise and lower the tricky dragon to make him difficult to slay. After each princess has a turn, let the Birthday Princess try again. This time, let her slay the dragon! Keep a sharp knife to weaken the seams if the piñata is too difficult to break, and be sure to set aside some goodies for the younger princesses that aren't fast enough to gather their own.

PRINCESS CRAFTS

NO-SEW PRINCESS SKIRTS

- Several 25-yard spools of 6-inch tulle in pastel colors
- One spool of ½-inch-wide white elastic
- Spools of ½-inch satin ribbon

(Each skirt will require 25 yards of tulle and 24 inches of elastic.)

Before the party, cut the tulle into 3-foot strips. During the party, stretch a piece of elastic around each girl's waist (not too tightly), trim, and tie into a knot. Have the girls choose 25 strips of tulle from the basket. Show them how to find the center of the first piece of tulle, and tie it onto their elastic waistband in a double knot, so that the knot has two equal length *legs*. Continue tying the rest of the pieces of tulle onto the waistbands in double knots. When you're finished, slide the knots around the waistband to space them evenly. Tie a few lengths of ribbon to the elastic between the tulle strips.

SWEET CASTLES

The day before the party, have your teenage helper construct an example castle with sugar cubes and canned frosting. The day of the party, mix food coloring into several bowls of white canned frosting, (pink, light blue, purple, etc.) Gather the princesses around the table, and hand each a paper plate, a pop-sicle stick, and several sugar cubes. Spread frosting on the plate so the first layer of cubes sticks in place. For the rest of the layers, dip the cubes into the frosting bowls and stack. Use sugarcoated gumdrops around the top. Add candy hearts, Smarties, and black licorice nib windows. Spread a bit of frosting around the bottom of the castle and sprinkle with green colored sugar crystals for grass, or blue colored crystals for a moat.

PRINCESS HATS

- Pastel, cone party hats
- Various stick-on gems
- Glitter glue pens
- Markers
- Ribbon

Set your supplies in the middle of the craft table and hand each princess a party hat. Have the girls decorate their hats with stickers, markers, and glitter glue. When the princesses are finished, tie three or four lengths of ribbon together in one knot. Snip off the point of the hat with a pair of scissors, and feed the unknotted ends through the hole from the inside.

FAIRY TISSUE FLOWERS

Before the party, cut pastel sheets of tissue paper into 6"x 6" squares. During the party, let the princesses choose six squares. Show them how to put the squares in a stack, and make one-inch accordion folds. Use scissors to cut both ends of the tissue strip to round the corners. Pinch the center of the tissue strip. Fold a pipe cleaner over the pinch, and secure it by twisting the ends together tightly. Fan-open both sides of the tissue paper. Gently pull each of the six layers of tissue, up and towards the center to form the flower's petals. Make larger flowers with 12" x 12" tissue.

FAIRY BUTTERFLIES

Pick up some pretty, brightly colored craft paper or wallpaper. Before the party, cut a stack of 2½-inch squares. Trim the two opposing sides of the squares to round them. Cutting will be easier if you create a template out of cardstock and trace the shape onto the back of the paper. On party day, gather the princesses around the table, and demonstrate how to accordion-fold each square into ¼ inch sections. Make sure the rounded sides are on the edges and the creases are sharp. Fold a 6-inch pipe cleaner in half and tuck two accordion-folded *wings* into the fold. Twist the ends together close to the wings to make antennae. Gently pull the wings apart on each side.

CHAPTER 10

THE COMPLETE GUIDE TO A JUNGLE SAFARI!

In the jungle, the mighty jungle, my mom planned a cool party! Whether from the plains of Africa or the Amazon rainforest, wild animals have always captured children's imaginations. So, put on some bug spray and take them on an animal adventure!

JUNGLE SAFARI INVITES

TOY JEEPS OR BINOCULARS

Plastic binoculars and safari jeeps are inexpensive and easy to find. Check your dollar store or shop online. Use raffia or twine to attach the Invite Tags.

SAFARI PALS

Grab an armful of wild beanbag animals at your local dollar store. Tie black ribbon around their necks, and use a hole-punch to attach an Invite Tag.

REAL COCONUTS

These are readily available at most grocery stores. Use scissors to trim the excess hair on the coconuts. Locate the three stem spots on the coconut, and create a funny face with a permanent marker. Tie a length of raffia or twine around each one. Handwrite or print your Invites on parchment paper, four per sheet. (This will make them small enough to attach to the coconuts.) Cut apart and roll them up. Attach another piece of raffia through the first piece and around the invite. Then, tie a bow. Tell your guests to bring their coconuts!

Here's an example of how you might word your Jungle Safari Invite:

> Through the dark jungle, filled with tall trees,
> I'm taking a trip. Will you join me?
> We'll spy on the hippos, and talk to some apes,
> Play jokes on tigers then make our escape!
> Meet at Ben's house on the 20th of June
> Don't miss the fun! It starts around NOON!
> 7735 Main Street – RSVP 555 5555

JUNGLE SAFARI FAVORS

Plastic canteens, boxes of animal crackers, bug catchers, binoculars, bamboo whistles, paddleballs, slap bracelets, pith helmets, straw safari hats, clip-on animal tails, safari vests, and Barrel of Monkeys games make great Jungle Safari favors.

FAVOR BAGS

The internet offers many options for jungle Safari favor bags: animal print lunch bags or take-out containers, camouflage hip packs, or drawstring net bags. Look for sites that sell by the dozen, and remember to allow enough time for shipping.

Jungle Safari Decorations

Follow the Paw Prints

Use colored chalk or washable paint to make elephant, tiger, bird and monkey foot prints on your sidewalk. You can also cut footprints out of black construction paper and secure them to the concrete with duct tape. See if the kids can figure out what kind of animals left the tracks. (If you're not sure what they look like, there are charts available online.)

Welcome to the Jungle

Lighted, inflatable, or jointed palm trees will help set the scene. If possible, move all your houseplants into the Party Room for the day. Ask your friends and neighbors if they have silk palms and ferns you can use. (Don't borrow live plants. You don't want to be responsible for their well-being!)

Table Covers

Raid your linen closet for plain tan flat sheets. Top them with animal print tissue paper, or burlap from the fabric store. Pick up some bamboo placemats at the dollar store. Decorate the tables with raffia, wood beads, beanbag wild animals, and rubber snakes. You can also use real coconuts, bunches of bananas and giant silk palm leaves to decorate the tables and snack buffet. Re-use the coconuts to play Coconut Bowling, or crack them open as an activity. After the party, peel and freeze the bananas to use in smoothies or banana bread.

Mosquito Netting

Any sheer lightweight white fabric will do. Check the clearance table at your local fabric store. Use it to accent colored tablecloths or hang panels from the ceiling to hide bookcases and electronics. It's also great for blocking off restricted areas.

TIKI TORCHES

Even if your Jungle Safari Party takes place during the day, Tiki torches can add jungle charm to the celebration. Line up a few torches along your driveway or sidewalk. Use them inside to accent large potted plants or zip-tie them to columns, poles and banisters.

PAPER VINES

What's a jungle without meandering vines? Twisted paper ribbon is an awesome and inexpensive way to bring the jungle indoors for your party. This versatile crafting staple is sometimes called *crinkle ribbon*, and looks like a thick cord when purchased. After you untwist it and pull it apart, it becomes 6-inch wide sturdy, wrinkled paper ribbon. There are dozens of colors to choose from, but green and brown will make the most realistic looking vines. If you can't find it locally, order some online. You can get 200 yards for less than ten dollars.

Untwisting the ribbon can take some time depending upon how much you plan to use. Cut the length you need before you pull it apart. This will make the process go faster. Once it's untwisted, roll it into useable coils until you're ready to decorate. The ribbon is a bit too heavy to secure with tape, so make sure you have thumbtacks handy.

Now that you have your ribbon untwisted, you can use it for a ton of things! Hang it like streamers from corner to corner in your Party Room; wrap stair railings and porch columns; use partially untwisted ribbon to hang vines from your ceiling fan or light fixtures; tie bows around the backs of the party chairs; or use it for the Man-Eating Vines Game (See Activities Section).

TARZAN SWINGS

Secure some thick cotton swinging ropes in a tall sturdy tree. Tie a few knots at the bottom to hold onto while you swing!

OUTDOOR JUNGLE SAFARI

A warm summer night is perfect for hosting an outdoor Jungle Safari Party! If you decide to do this, Tiki torches are mandatory. Place torches around the perimeter of the party, and use them to illuminate dark sidewalks and pathways. You might also want to light a few citronella candles at night. They do double-duty controlling mosquitoes and casting warm light around the party. Remember that torch fuel and citronella candles are both highly toxic, so keep them away from food and children.

BUILD a FIRE the general idea

If you don't have the desire or ability to dig your own fire pit, a store-bought fire pit will work just fine. These shallow metal bowls usually sit off the ground in a small frame. Borrow one from a neighbor or friend. Or, purchase one at your local supercenter. (You can always re-use it for block parties and campouts.) As with any fire, make sure the area is flat and clear of leaves and debris. Store-bought firewood works best in fire pits because it is already cut to a usable size. Fire-starter logs are great for ambience, but should not be used to roast marshmallows. They contain harmful chemicals that will transfer to your food.

JUNGLE SOUNDS

Inside or out, you cannot have a Jungle Safari Party without the sounds of the jungle. Download or pick up some recorded nature sounds (tropical birds or music.)

OTHER ITEMS TO CONSIDER:

Stuffed parrots and tropical birds can be hung from the ceiling. Giant rubber or stuffed snakes can wind their way through the snack buffet. (Make your own with dark green tights stuffed with tissue paper.) Add some plastic pink flamingos to your front yard; your neighbors will love you!

JUNGLE SAFARI FOOD

PIRANHA BUFFET

Line up several glass fishbowls. Tie raffia around each rim, and fill with animal crackers, dried banana chips, grapes, carrot sticks, Chex Mix, peanuts in the shell, boxes of raisins, and of course, Fruit Loops.

MOSQUITO MELONS

Use a melon baller to scoop balls of cantaloupe, watermelon and honey dew. Arrange by color on a round tray. Start in the middle with pink watermelon. Add a row of orange cantaloupe, and then add a row of green honeydew around the cantaloupe. Repeat until the tray is full, and add fun jungle cocktail picks.

SAVAGE SAUSAGES

Easy peasy! Mix a bag of cocktail weenies and BBQ sauce into a snack-size Crock-Pot. Serve with cocktail picks or toothpicks.

JUNGLE WRAPS

Wash and dry some lettuce leaves. Lay one leaf flat and top with a slice of turkey, a dab of ranch dressing, and a slice of American cheese. Roll lettuce leaf tightly and secure with two cocktail picks. Slice in half with a plastic knife (to prevent wilting). Refrigerate until the party, and serve on a platter with giant silk palm leaves.

PANTHER POCKETS

The morning of the party, combine ground turkey or hamburger and shredded cheese in a large bowl. Form into oblong patties that will fit into mini-pita pockets. Grill the patties on the BBQ pit, and place into a warm oven until the guests arrive. When it's time to eat, stuff each patty into a pita pocket, and top with shredded lettuce, BBQ sauce, ketchup, or mustard. Serve with dried shoestring potatoes.

PARROT PINWHEELS

- Carrots
- Red peppers
- Zucchini
- Yellow squash
- Dry Ranch dip
- Cream cheese
- Sour cream
- Tortillas

The night before the party, use a large-hole box grater to shred the vegetables. Add the shredded vegetables, a brick of cream cheese, ¼ cup of sour cream, and the packet of dry Ranch dip to a gallon size plastic zipper bag. Remove the air and zip the bag closed. Mix the ingredients by smooshing the bag from the outside. When thoroughly combined, smooth a ¼-inch thick layer onto each flour tortilla. Roll the tortillas tightly, and wrap in clear plastic wrap. Refrigerate until the party. Use a sharp knife to slice the rolls into ½-inch spirals, and serve them a platter covered with dry, green leafy lettuce. What a great way to get kids to eat vegetables!

FIRE ANTS ON A LOG

A kid's snack classic with a twist. Cut some celery stalks into 6-inch pieces. Fill celery *logs* with cream cheese spread or peanut butter. Top with dried cranberry *fire ants*.

ELEPHANT SANDWICHES

Peel and dice several bananas into ½-inch pieces. Fold diced bananas into a bowl of creamy peanut butter. Lay eight slices of bread on the counter. Use a rubber spatula to smooth a layer of the mixture onto each slice. Stack one prepared slice on top of another (peanut butter-banana side up). Add a third slice of bread to make a triple-decker elephant-sized sandwich. Use a sharp knife to slice the sandwiches twice diagonally (to make four triangles). Skewer with cocktail picks, cover with plastic wrap, and refrigerate until the party.

Jungle Safari Desserts

Gorilla Popsicles

- Bananas
- Peanut butter
- Strawberry jam
- Cheerios
- Pop-sicle sticks

The night before the party, peel several bananas, cut in half crosswise, and insert pop-sicle sticks into the cut ends. Combine equal parts of peanut butter and jam in a bowl. Mix well, and spread onto the bananas. Roll each banana in a plate of Cheerios to coat all sides. Place the coated bananas on a wax paper-covered cookie sheet and freeze. Thaw at room temperature for 10 minutes before serving.

Tiger Stripe Cookies

- Roll of sugar cookie dough
- Tootsie Rolls
- Orange sugar crystals
- Waxed paper

Microwave several Tootsie Rolls to soften (less than six seconds), and place the softened candy between two pieces of waxed paper. Use a rolling pin to flatten to 1/8-inch thick, and slice into tiger stripes with a sharp knife. Repeat until you have enough for five or six stripes per cookie. Refrigerate the stripes on a cookie sheet. Bake cookies as directed and move them to a wire rack. While the cookies are still warm, arrange the candy stripes on each cookie and sprinkle with orange sugar crystals.

Biscuit Monkey Bread

- Sugar
- Cinnamon
- Butter
- Four cans of biscuits

In a saucepan, melt 1/3 cup of sugar, 2 tsp cinnamon, and two sticks of butter. Boil for two minutes. Open four cans of biscuits, and cut each biscuit into four pieces. In a bowl, combine 1 cup of sugar and 1 tsp cinnamon. Roll each biscuit piece in the mixture, and then layer in a greased Bundt pan. Cover the biscuits with the boiled sauce. Bake at 350 for 30 minutes. Cool 15 minutes, and then turn onto a serving plate. Serve warm.

CHEETAH CAKE

- Yellow cake mix
- Box of chocolate pudding
- Yellow food coloring
- Whipped topping
- Chocolate chips

Bake the yellow cake as directed in a 9x13-glass casserole. Let cool completely. Punch holes in the cake about one inch apart with a wooden spoon. Prepare the chocolate pudding according to box, and pour over the cake. Use a rubber spatula to coax the pudding into the holes. Spread the remaining pudding evenly over the top. Let cool in the refrigerator for 20 minutes. Mix a few drops of yellow food coloring into a container of whipped topping, and spread over the pudding cake. Sprinkle with chocolate chips and return to the refrigerator until you're ready to serve.

PEANUT BUTTER ZEBRA POOP

- One-14 oz can of sweetened condensed milk (not evaporated milk)
- 48 Hershey Hugs
- 3/4 cup creamy peanut butter
- 2 cups of Bisquik
- 1 teaspoon of vanilla extract
- 1/4 cup sugar

Pre-heat the oven to 375. Beat sweetened condensed milk and peanut butter in large bowl until smooth. Add baking mix and vanilla; blend well. Shape into one-inch balls; roll in sugar. Place 2 inches apart on cookie sheets, and bake 6 to 8 minutes or until light brown. Remove from oven, and immediately press a Hug into center of each ball. Transfer the cookies to a wire rack to cool. Store them in an airtight container until the party. These treats will disappear in the blink of an eye so make sure you bake extra!

JUNGLE SAFARI DRINKS

JUNGLE JUICE

- Orange juice
- Cranberry juice
- Lemon-lime soda
- Oranges
- Maraschino cherries

To make an ice ring, slice oranges (with skin) into ½-inch thick cross-wise sections. Add a drained jar of cherries to the bottom of a small, round, plastic chip server (the kind with space in the middle for dip). Layer orange slices on top of the cherries. Cover with cranberry juice and freeze overnight. As guests arrive, pour orange juice, lemon-lime soda and cranberry juice (2-2-1 ratio) into a punch bowl. Run warm water over the bottom of the ice ring to release from plastic, and add it to the punch. Serve in plastic coconuts. If you can't make an ice ring, just freeze ice trays filled with cherries and cranberry juice.

FRUIT SMOOTHIES

Gather assorted juices, milk, chocolate syrup, bananas, oranges, blueberries, strawberries, canned pineapple chunks, etc. (Never mix fresh pineapple with milk; it curdles in your stomach!). Set a blender on the counter and let the kids choose their poison! Serve in tall glasses with colorful straws and Maraschino cherries. Popular flavor combos: Pineapple-Banana, Chocolate-strawberry, and Peanut Butter-Banana.

JUNGLE SAFARI ACTIVITIES

COCONUT BOWLING

Set up empty tin cans or 1/2 gallon milk jugs as pins. Use real coconuts for bowling balls. This is a fun activity to play inside or outdoors.

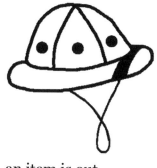

GOING ON A SAFARI

Have the players sit in a circle. The first player says, *I'm going on a safari, and I'm going to pack...bug spray.* Then the next player says, *I'm going on a safari and I'm going to pack bug spray and ...binoculars.* Repeating the first player's item and adding their own. Play continues around the circle. Any player that forgets an item is out.

OPEN REAL COCONUTS

Kids (even teenagers) love this! Use the drain opening of your kitchen sink to hold the coconut while you puncture two of the *eyes* with a corkscrew or a cordless drill with a ¼-inch bit. Let the coconuts drain in the sink. (It's not coconut milk. It's mostly water. Coconut milk is a processed product.) After draining, wrap the coconut in a towel and place the point of the coconut (where the three eyes are) on a concrete floor or sidewalk. Strike the bottom of the coconut firmly with a hammer. The nut should crack open easily. Bake the pieces on a cookie sheet at 350 for about 15 minutes to make the meat easier to remove from the shell. Eat raw or use a cheese grater to make flakes, and pop them back in the oven to toast.

CHEETAH CHATTER

You'll need a stuffed cheetah to play this game! Have the players sit in a circle. Choose one player to sit in the middle to be the blindfolded *chatterer*. Choose a topic (candy bars, TV shows, cereal, movies, etc.). When you say, *go*, the person in the middle must list as many things as they can from the topic. While they are chattering, the cheetah is passed around the circle. The *chatterer* yells *stop* when they can't think of anymore. Whoever has the cheetah becomes the chatterer. The blindfold keeps the chatterer from choosing who goes next.

HUMAN KNOTS

Have the players stand close in a circle. To begin, everyone puts their right hand into the center of the circle and takes hold of someone else's right hand. Repeat the process with their left hands. The object of the game is to see if they can untangle the knot by turning around, stepping over, or ducking under without letting go!

MOSQUITO BITES

Pass out sheet of small, red dot stickers (mosquito bites) as the kids arrive. The object of the game is to get rid of all stickers. Secretly place stickers (bites) on the other players when they are not paying attention. If you are caught, you have to wear your own *bite*. If you are *bit* by someone else, you have to keep the sticker on until the end of the game. The first player to get rid of all of their stickers wins!

SAFARI SNAPSHOTS

Have a variety of pith helmets, khaki T-shirts, binoculars, safari vests, stuffed snakes, toy cameras, maps, and other safari items on hand. Let each kid dress up and pose for the camera. Use jungle animal cutouts and palm trees to make a backdrop. Insert copies of the photos in with your Thank You cards!

MAN EATING VINES

Grab some green and brown streamers and tape. While you busy the kids with another activity, have your teenage party helper attach *vines* from wall to wall around the Party Room. The object of the game is to get from one side of the room to the other. As players walk through, they can't touch the *vines* with any part of their body; they have to crawl under or jump over them. If you touch them, you're out. The first player to cross the room wins!

PEANUT PUSHERS

Use masking tape to mark a starting line and a finish line 8 to 10 feet apart on a carpeted surface. Have the players form a line, side-by-side. Place a peanut (in the shell) on the starting line in front of each player. When you say *go*, the players push their peanuts toward the finish line using only their noses and faces.

MUSICAL HIPPO HOP

This is a fun jungle version of musical chairs. Set up several pillows in a circle; leave 4-5 feet between each pillow. Put one less pillow than there are players. Start playing music, and have the players hop around the circle, (landing on a pillow and then two hops on the floor) until the music stops. When the music stops, the players must each plop down on a pillow. The child without a pillow, *fell in the water*, and has to sit in the middle. Remove another pillow. If there is ever a tie, the player with more tush on the pillow gets to keep playing. The giggles will get louder as you remove pillows, the circle gets smaller, and the players get closer to the kids *in the water*!

JUNGLE SUCKER

Each player has a plate filled with animal crackers, an empty plate, and a straw. When you say *go*, the players have two minutes to suck the Animal Crackers onto their straw (so that the suction keeps the cracker attached to the bottom of the straw), and move them to the empty plate. Whoever gets them all moved first, wins!

JUNGLE SAFARI CRAFTS

AFRICAN DRUMS

- Round empty oatmeal containers
- Jungle print wrapping paper
- Tape
- String

Take the lids off and wrap the containers in a fun safari print. Poke a hole on either side to insert a knotted carry strap (string). Replace the lid! Drum away!

JUNGLE MASKS

- Paper plates
- Colored tissue paper
- Glue sticks and hot glue gun
- Construction paper
- Drink straws
- Scissors
- Markers

Here are a few ideas to get started:

LIONS- Tear light brown tissue into one-inch wide strips. Use the glue stick to attach the strips around the perimeter of the paper plate for a mane. Tear light brown tissue into one-inch pieces, and glue around the inside of the mane, overlapping as you go. Repeat with rows of overlapping pieces of orange tissue. Fill the center with pieces of yellow tissue. Add oval eyes, a nose, a mouth, and whiskers cut from black construction paper, and hot glue a straw to the back as a handle.

ELEPHANTS- Cover the plate with one-inch gray tissue pieces. Cut a J-shaped nose, and long oval ears out of gray construction paper. Add round eyes cut from black construction paper, and hot glue a straw to the back as a handle.

TIGERS- Cover the plate with one-inch orange tissue pieces. Cut long triangles of black construction paper, and glue them as tiger stripes along either side, (with the triangle tips pointing toward the center). Add oval eyes, a nose, a mouth, and whiskers cut from black construction paper, and hot glue a straw to the back as a handle.

ZEBRAS- Cover the plate with one-inch white tissue pieces. Attach vertical, black construction paper stripes, wide-set black eyes, and a nose, and hot glue a straw to the back as a handle.

FROGS- Cut a large oval out of green construction paper. Glue it to the front of the paper plate. Trace the bottom of a plastic cup to cut out two eyes, and glue them to the top of the oval. Add a giant smile to the front with markers, and hot glue a straw to the back as a handle.

BINOCULARS

- Paper towel tubes
- Stapler
- Hole-punch
- String
- Electrical tape
- Scissors

Cut each paper towel tube in half. Let the kids each cover the outside of two tubes with black electrical tape. Use a stapler to attach them in the middle. (Two staples in each end.) Use the hole-punch to add a hole to the outside of either side of the binoculars. Add a length of string tying the knots on the inside.

RAINSTICKS

- 6-inch cardboard mailing tubes with end caps
- Aluminum foil
- Markers, stickers
- Un-popped popcorn
- Dry beans
- Dry rice

Gather all of the supplies on the table. Hand each kid a mailing tube. Demonstrate how to make the rain tubes. Put the cap on one end of the tube. Cut a piece of aluminum foil six inches wide and 12 inches long. Crumple the foil into two long snakes. Twist the foil snakes into the shape of a spring. Put the springs into the tube. Add popcorn, beans, and rice. Seal closed with the other plastic cap. Decorate with stickers and markers.

CHAPTER 11

THE COMPLETE GUIDE TO AN OUTER SPACE PARTY!

Whether the Birthday Kid loves exploring the wonders of outer space, or just loves the idea of slimy aliens, an Outer Space Party can be a blast!

OUTER SPACE INVITES

MOON ROCKS
Gather several empty baby food jars, and some gumball-size craggy rocks. Spray paint the jar lids and the rocks with silver spray paint. When the moon rocks are dry, place one inside each jar. Add one inch of fine white sand from the craft store. Attach Invite Tags with silver prism curling ribbon.

FREEZE-DRIED ICE CREAM
Give your guests a taste of what real astronauts eat! Single-serving bags of freeze-dried ice cream are available in the camping dept of most supercenters or sporting goods stores. Staple Invites to the top of each bag!

ALIENS

Stuffed aliens and aliens in test tubes are easy to find at the dollar store, supercenter or online. Attach Invite Tags with silver ribbon.

Here's an example of how you might word your Outer Space Party Invite:

> COME, JOIN OUR ADVENTURE AS WE BLAST OFF TO SPACE!
> OUR PRE-FLIGHT TRAINING WILL BEGIN AT BEN'S PLACE.
> REPORT FOR DUTY AUGUST 21 AT NOON
> WE'LL HAVE ASTRONAUT SNACKS, AND CHECK OUT THE MOON!
> 7735 MAIN STREET- 555-5555

COOL TIP!

If you are making hand written invitations or Invite Tags, use silver marker or white pencil on black or navy blue paper. Trim the edges with zigzag scissors.

OUTER SPACE PARTY FAVORS

Foam rocket slingshots, Milky Way bars, Mars bars, Starburst, Pop Rocks, Orbit gum, blacklight pens, Slinkys, and alien antenna headbands make great Outer Space party favors! Make your own favor bags out of bubble wrap and duct tape!

GLOW-IN-THE-DARK FAVORS

If you're using blacklights in the party room, glow-in-the-dark sticks, bracelets, necklaces, rings, and beads are a must!

ID BADGE FAVORS

Pick up some plastic, clip-on ID badges or lanyards at the office supply store. Use your computer to add each kid's name and photo (ask the parents to email a photo). Give them job titles like *Navigation Specialist, Flight Controller, Orbital Operations, Communications Specialist, Environmental Manager, and Propulsion Engineer*. Add words like *NASA Mission Control, and Security Clearance Alpha*.

SPACE SUIT FAVORS

White, disposable coveralls are available online, and make the perfect astronaut suits. Order the smallest size. Roll up or trim the sleeves and legs. Use fabric paint to add details like stripes on the sleeves or the astronauts' names across the back, and iron American Flag patches on the sleeves.

ALIEN SCANNING DEVICES

Collect several old, un-used TV, stereo, or VCR remote controls from your neighbors and friends. Paint them with silver spray paint. Pass them out to the kids to use as alien detectors, communication devices, or atmospheric scanners! (Don't forget to remove the batteries.)

OUTER SPACE DECORATIONS

By far, the best place to hold an Outer Space Party is in your garage. It's a nice open space. There are few windows to cover, and attaching things to the ceiling isn't as devastating as it would be inside.

CARDBOARD PLANETS

- Cardboard
- Pencil on a string
- Glow-in-the-dark paint

Easy peasy! Hold the string in the center of your circle. Pull the string taunt and trace a circle with the pencil. (For smaller planets, trace a pot lid or plate.) Cut out the planets and paint both sides with glow-in-the-dark paint, and let dry. Unfold half of a paper clip and poke one end through the cardboard planet. Attach fishing line to the other end to hang.

PLANETARY SOLAR SYSTEM

What's an Outer Space Party without planets? Depending upon whom you talk to, there are either eight or nine planets in our solar system. (Pluto being the bone of contention.) The others are Mercury, Venus, Earth, Mars, Neptune, Saturn, Jupiter, and Uranus. There are several simple ways to make planets for the party. I'll let you decide if you want to include Pluto or not.

TWINKLING STARS

Hang several strands of white mini-lights across the ceiling. (The more the better!) If you don't have any, ask your neighbor or friends to dig through their Christmas decorations; even the *icicle* mini-lights will work. If you're also using blacklights, keep the twinkling stars off until you need more light for food or activities.

BLACKLIGHTS, BLACKLIGHTS, BLACKLIGHTS!

There isn't an easier way to transform your Party Room than to switch out your regular light bulbs blacklights. Under a true blacklight, white and light colored fabrics will glow, and neon colors will dazzle. Cover any windows with black construction paper, or black trash bags to enhance the effect. These bulbs can be found at your local hardware store for a few dollars each.

NOTE:

Make sure that the blacklight bulbs you buy are the compact florescent (squiggly tube) bulbs, and NOT incandescent (regular shaped) bulbs. Regardless of what the package says, regular shaped blacklight bulbs give off purple light, and do not make things glow beyond a few inches. A 13-watt compact florescent (CF) blacklight bulb will fit any standard incandescent socket, and has a glow range of 6-8 feet. If your garage lights use long florescent tubes, you can replace them with florescent black lights, but they are more expensive, and a bit harder to find. If your garage has no overhead lights, consider hanging a few handyman droplights with CF blacklight bulbs.

PAPER MACHE PLANETS

- Round balloons
- Newspaper
- Flour or white glue
- Water
- Glow in the dark paint
- White printer paper

Regular balloons will make oval planets, so check your craft store for round balloons. The weekend before the party, tear the newspaper into 2-inch strips. In a large bowl, mix a batch of paste. (Three parts white glue to one part water, or equal parts flour and water.) Blow up several balloons in varying sizes. Use a bowl to stabilize the round balloon as you cover it. Dip the newspaper strips into the paste and apply the strips to the balloons, criscrossing along the way. 12-inch newspaper strips are easiest to handle. After you add three layers of newspaper, tear white printer paper into 2-inch strips to use for the last layer. (This will take a few coats of paint to cover.) Let the *planets* dry completely before painting (24-48 hours). Coat the planets with different color glow-in-the-dark paint. When dry, hang from the ceiling with fishing line tied to the balloons' knots.

DID YOU KNOW?

All of the giant planets in our solar system (Jupiter, Saturn, Uranus, and Neptune) have rings, but Saturn's rings are the easiest to see? Use a permanent marker to add an authentic ring around your Saturn balloon planet.

METALLIC TWIST RIBBON

This versatile crafting staple is sometimes called "crinkle ribbon", and looks like a thick cord when purchased. After you untwist it and pull it apart, it becomes a 4-6 inch wide wrinkled ribbon that's reflective like aluminum foil, but doesn't tear as easily. (I think it's actually made from thin-coated plastic, so you'll definitely need scissors.) Metallic twist ribbon is available at most craft stores in 25-foot lengths. (If you can't find it locally or need a larger quantity, check online where you can find 300-yard spools for less than fifty dollars.) The durability of this ribbon makes it perfect for hanging in strips as a door curtain to the Party Room. It can also be hung as streamers, or wrapped around railings and beams.

I SEE STARS

Print, or use a star-shaped cookie cutter to trace stars onto cardstock. Cut out and cover with aluminum foil. Attach a paper clip to the top point of each, and hang with fishing line and thumbtacks. This is a great project for the Birthday Kid!

WHITE SHEETS

Cover the walls and hide shelving with plain white sheets from your linen closet. The bright white will glow in the blacklights. If they look too plain, use safety pins to add aluminum foil covered stars.

NEON PAINT

Glow-in-the-dark or neon craft paint can be used for just about anything! Use it to paint your Paper Mache or cardboard planets. If you're covering the garage walls with canvas tarps or white sheets, use the neon paint to decorate them with shooting stars and nebulas. Make cardboard cutouts of alien beings and space ships. Cover them with neon paint that will glow under the blacklights.

ALUMINUM FOIL

Foil is just as versatile as neon paint. Cover a few cardboard shoeboxes to make space shuttle control panels. Add spray-painted bottle tops as knobs. Wrap Birthday presents in foil instead of wrapping paper. In fact, go all out and wrap everything you can in aluminum foil!

COOL IDEA!

Stop by your local teachers' store. The science department will have a ton of great space-themed decorating ideas.

OUTER SPACE FOOD

ALIEN SNACK BUFFET
Line up several glass fishbowls, fill and label them with *planets* (black, red, and green seedless grapes), *space ships* (peanut butter filled Ritz Bits), *alien guts* (kiwi and strawberry slices), *black holes* (chocolate Cheerios), mini-Milky Way bars, Starburst, Sun Chips, etc.

YOGURT AND PUDDING TUBES!
Snack just like the astronauts! Pick up these fun treats in the refrigerated section of your grocery store. Try them frozen!

COOL IDEA!
Serve all the food and snacks on aluminum pie plates or potpie tins!

GRAVITY-DEFYING BACON AND MAC BOWLS
The morning of the party, pre-heat the oven to 400. Open two, one-pound packages of thick-sliced, quality bacon. (The cheap stuff has too much fat.) Turn a large muffin pan upside-down. Yes, upside down! Cut the slices of bacon in half, and form T-shapes over each of the inverted cups. Wrap two slices of bacon around each cup, weaving in and out of the T-shaped pieces. Spiral another strip around the outside of the bacon *basket* on each cup. (If necessary, secure with a wooden toothpick.) Place in the oven. Add a deep cookie sheet on the rack below to catch all the drippings. (There will be a lot!) Bake 45 minutes or until the bowls are crispy and brown. Let cool and invert onto a paper towel until you're ready to serve. Prepare a regular box of macaroni and cheese as directed, and spoon into the bacon bowls to serve.

COSMIC PINWHEELS

- Carrots
- Red peppers
- Zucchini
- Yellow squash
- Dry Ranch dip
- Cream cheese
- Sour cream
- Tortillas

The night before the party, use a large-hole box grater to shred the vegetables. Add the shredded vegetables, a brick of cream cheese, ¼ cup of sour cream, and the packet of dry Ranch dip to a gallon size plastic zipper bag. Remove the air and zip the bag closed. Mix the ingredients by smooshing the bag from the outside. When thoroughly combined, smooth a ¼-inch thick layer onto each flour tortilla. Roll the tortillas tightly, and wrap in clear plastic wrap. Refrigerate until the party. Use a sharp knife to slice the rolls into ½-inch spirals, and serve them on a platter covered with dry, green leafy lettuce. Meat and cheese pinwheels can be made with the same technique. Substitute the shredded vegetables with diced ham or turkey and shredded cheese.

NIGHT SKY SANDWICHES

Make regular peanut butter and jelly, or ham and cheese sandwiches on white or wheat sandwich bread. Use star, circle, and moon-shaped cookie cutters to trim the sandwiches into space shapes.

REAL ASTRONAUT FOOD

Stop by your local camping store, and browse through their selection of dehydrated meals. Everything from spaghetti and meatballs to peach cobbler (and of course, freeze-dried ice cream) can be found with little effort. Buy a variety, and let the kids taste-test all of them. Follow the directions on the packages. Most freeze-dried meals require hot water for preparation. Let the kids eat them right out of the bags!

SATELLITE SNACKS

Fill dollar roll buns with tuna, egg, or ham salad. Add pretzel sticks for antennas, and sensors.

ALIEN NACHOS

Fill a snack-size Crock-Pot with nacho cheese (Velveeta), salsa, and green food coloring. Use a divided snack tray to serve toppings: salsa, guacamole, diced tomatoes, sour cream, and jalapeño peppers. Pre-fill bowls with tortilla chips to prevent waste.

OUTER SPACE DESERTS

Moon Pies; Little Debbie's brand Star Crunch treats, Bomb Pops, homemade snow cones, or candy bars like Milky Way and Mars bars. Easy peasy!

MOON LANDING CAKE

- White cake mix
- Can of white frosting
- Oreo cookies
- Necco candy wafers, etc.

Bake the cake as directed in a 13 x 9 casserole. Let cool. Finely crush the cookies in a plastic zipper bag and add them to the frosting. Frost the cake with a serving spoon to make mountains, craters, and valleys. Add gray Necco candy wafers as craters; Use a toy GI Joe boot dipped in powdered sugar to make Moon landing footprints; Add a paper American flag toothpick; Cut the neck off of a plastic funnel and cover with aluminum foil for a space capsule!

GLOW IN THE DARK JELLO

Prepare a few boxes of any flavor gelatin, substituting tonic water for regular water. Refrigerate until firm. Use cookie cutters to cut out shapes. Shine a black light on the gelatin to make it glow. No matter what flavor or color you use, the gelatin will glow bright blue under a black light. This is the fluorescence of the Quinine in the tonic water. Quinine also gives tonic water a distinctive bitter flavor that you might taste in the gelatin. You can lessen this bitterness by using half-tonic water and half-tap water in the recipe.

MARS-MALLOW CRISPY TREATS

Melt ½ stick of butter and 6 cups of mini-marshmallows in a large pot. Stir until melted. Add 8 cups of Rice Crispies Cereal and mix with a rubber spatula. Pour mixture into a 13 x 9 greased glass casserole. Let cool and cut into squares. Add red food coloring to the marshmallow mixture to make the crispy treats red like the planet Mars!

OUTER SPACE DRINKS

ALIEN PUNCH

Mix equal parts green drink mix, and lemon-lime soda. Pour into a punch bowl. The night before the party, fill ice cube trays with green drink mix and Maraschino cherries.

ASTEROID SODAS

Call around to your local grocery stores to see which one carries frozen ice cream beads (a.k.a. Dippin' Dots). They're out there; you just have to look. When you're ready to serve, pour into clear plastic cocktail cups and cover with root beer. Try different flavor combinations depending on what's available, chocolate with strawberry soda, vanilla with cola, or banana split with cream soda.

DON'T FORGET THE TANG!

OUTER SPACE INDOOR ACTIVITIES

REMOTE CONTROL ROVER

Divide the players into teams of two. As each team takes a turn, blindfold one of the players. Toss several throw pillows on the floor around the Party Room. The object of the game is for the controller to give commands to his rover, and help him walk his way through the obstacle course to the finish. Tell the kids to say commands like, *Take two steps to the left, rover*, and *take a step forward, rover,* etc. To make it more difficult, hang a few Paper Mache planets low enough so that rover will have to duck!

PLANET TWISTER

Before the party, stretch a flat white sheet on your garage floor. Use a large pot lid to trace circles all over the sheet with a permanent marker. Paint the circles different colors with craft paint, and label the circles with a planet's name. Write the planet's names on pieces of paper, fold them, and place them in a cup. Use a permanent marker to write the letters on a die (dice): RH (right hand) on two sides, LH (left hand) on two sides, RF (right foot) on one side, and LF (left foot) on one side. During the party, spread the sheet out on the carpet.

Let the players take turns rolling the die (dice), and choosing a planet out of the cup, then following the directions; *Put your RH (right hand) on Pluto*. Once the players are in play, roll the die, choose a planet for them, and call out their directions. If a player falls, they are out. The last player wins! Just like the original game, the fun is watching the kids get tangled up while attempting to reach the open spots! (With younger kids, no one is out if they fall. They just have to remember where their hands, and feet were. You can keep playing until they want to do something else.)

COOL IDEA!

If you want to be authentic paint the planets their true colors: Mercury- orange, Venus- yellow, Earth- blue, Mars- red, Jupiter-yellow, Uranus- green, Saturn- yellow, Neptune- blue, and Pluto- yellow.

STRAW ROCKET RACES

- Drinking straws
- Balloons
- Tape
- String
- Chairs

Cut fifteen 20-foot lengths of string. Divide the players into teams of two. Line chairs up on one side of the room. Tie one end of each string to the back of its own chair. Have the teams stretch their string back across the room to a starting line. Hand each team a balloon, a straw, and a piece of tape. The object of the game is for the players to work as a team to follow these steps: Blow up the balloon (hold it closed). Tape the balloon to the straw. Feed the string through the straw. Hold the string tight, and let the air out of their balloon, so that their straw and balloon race down their string to the finish line. The first team's straw to touch the line wins!

MOON ROCK RELAY

Before the party, gather a few dozen golf ball-size rocks. Paint the rocks with silver spray paint. Divide the players into two teams. Place two empty buckets 30-feet from the starting line, where you've made two piles of moon rocks. Hand the starting player from each team a pair of kitchen tongs. When you say *go*, the players must use the tongs to grab a moon rock, and slow-motion run to bucket and drop it in. Then, the players must slow-motion run back to the starting line and hand off their tongs to the next player on their team. The first team to move all of their moon rocks wins! (The hysterical part is watching the kids attempt to hurry while still moving in slow motion. Make sure to keep your digital or video camera handy!)

COLLECT THE METEORITES

Before the party, make a basket full of aluminum foil balls, in varying sizes. Hide them around the Party Room, or yard like Easter eggs. Give each child a paper bag, and let them loose collecting their meteorites! The player with the most wins a prize. For a fun twist, use waded balls of newspaper sprayed with glow-in-the-dark paint. Conduct the search in a dark room!

OUTER SPACE OUTDOOR ACTIVITIES

SATURN RING TOSS

- Several empty boxes or buckets
- String or masking tape
- A yellow, cardboard, or fabric Sun
- Plastic pool toy rings

Place the Sun in the middle of the solar system (yard). Use the string to make several rings, about one foot apart, around the Sun. (If possible, do this before the party to save time.) Place a bucket or box on each ring in varying directions. Let the players take turns standing on the Sun, and tossing rings into the buckets. Keep score and give more points for landing on the *planets* further away.

EARTH DEFENDER

Find a giant 36-inch Earth beach ball online, or paint a standard beach ball with blue and green craft paint to resemble the Earth. Place the beach ball on top of a 5-gallon bucket. Divide the players into two teams. The team defending Earth must stand in place around the Earth and only wave their arms to deflect any incoming meteors (12-inch beach balls) from the attacking team. If a meteor hits the Earth, the game is over, and the teams switch sides.

SPACESHIP RUNWAY

Lay three hula-hoops in a row about 20 feet from where the players are lined up. Let them take turns trying to land the *space ships* (Frisbees) in the hula-hoops. Give more points for space ships that land in the farthest hoop, and fewer points for the space ships that land in the closest hoop.

BOTTLE ROCKETS

If it's age appropriate, and in compliance with your town's ordinances, shoot off some bottle rockets in the backyard! Make sure the kids stand back while watching, and get parental approval before letting any child participate in the lighting of fireworks.

SPACE BLASTER BATTLE

Paint several hand-held water guns with silver spray paint. Divide the players into two teams: Aliens and Earthlings. No aiming for the head! Make sure you have your digital or video camera handy.

OUTER SPACE EVENING ACTIVITIES

GLOWING SODA COMET (AFTER DARK)

- One roll of Mentos candies
- One 1-liter bottle of tonic water
- Paper or cardboard
- A black light

Make sure the tonic water lists Quinine as an ingredient. (That's the stuff that makes it glow.) Remove the label from the bottle. Turn off exterior lights to make it as dark as possible. Place the black light close to the bottle, but still far enough away that it won't get wet. Unwrap the Mentos and stack them in a paper tube. Line up the tube with the open bottle of tonic. When everyone is ready, release the candies into the bottle, and stand back!

USE A TELESCOPE (AFTER DARK)

Of course! If you don't have one of your own, or you don't have a neighbor, friend, or relative that has one to lend, make a few calls to the higher end camera stores in your area. Many of these stores have telescopes you can rent. If not, simply grab a pair of binoculars. Once you have your viewing instrument, hop on the Internet, and search for sites that tell you what's in view in your area the night of the party. Make a list of several things to locate, and write down the general direction of where to start searching.

Turn the exterior lights off, and start scanning the sky. (Even if you live in the city, there is plenty to see in the night sky.) Believe it or not, all of the planets in our solar system can be seen at one time or another using a telescope; some are more difficult to see than others are, but they're all still there for the finding. Mars and Venus are the easiest to see, and Mercury is more difficult because of it's proximity to the Sun. If you can't find any planets, simply getting a closer look at the Moon can be fascinating.

Stir the kids' imaginations by asking what they think it would be like to actually land on the Moon. Would it be cold? Would it be scary? Would it be quiet? What would Earth look like? See if you can recognize any constellations, or find satellites in orbit. Sometimes, it might take a while to find what you're looking for, so make sure the kids have something to occupy their time while you focus the telescope. Pass out glow sticks, or throw a few blankets on the ground, and give each kid a print-out of easy to find constellations like the Big Dipper (due North), and Leo the Lion. Look due south; you might find Sagittarius, Scorpius, and even the Milky Way!

OUTER SPACE CRAFTS

MOON SHOES

Pick up some plastic shoeboxes (two per child), and a bag of 7" x 5/8" rubber bands. If you can't find large rubber bands at your office supply store, check out Uline.com. Let the kids stretch several rubber bands around the perimeter of each plastic shoebox, so that there is ¼ inch between each band. Have the kids take off their shoes (keeping socks on), and sit in a chair. Show them how to tuck their toes under three bands, and over three bands on the open side of the shoeboxes, (so they fit like slippers). Tell them to hold on to the table and stand up, and then bounce a little. Make sure the kids stay on the carpet when walking in their moon shoes to prevent injuries from falling.

JARS OF SPACE

- Baby food jars
- Silver glitter
- Star glitter
- Blue food coloring
- Hot glue
- Water

Easy peasy! Add a tablespoon of silver glitter, a teaspoon of star glitter, and several drops of blue food coloring to each jar. Add water to the jars until there is one-half inch remaining at the top of each. Replace the caps and add a bead of hot glue around the rim to prevent leaks. Let the kids add star and space stickers to the top.

ASTRONAUT GLOVE DRAWINGS

Let the kids see how hard it is to work in outer space while wearing a space suit! Give each child an oven mitt, or thick utility glove. Let them try to draw pictures with white chalk, or white crayons on black or blue construction paper.

HOMEMADE ROCKETS

- Plastic 35 mm film canisters (the kind where the lid fits inside the rim, not outside)
- Printer paper and cardstock
- Tape
- Scissors
- Alka-Seltzer tablets
- Paper towels
- Water

Cut the printer paper into 4"x6" strips. Add a piece of tape to one narrow end of the paper and attach it to the canister. Wrap the paper around the film canister, so that the lid end of the canister sticks out about one-eighth of an inch, and tape closed. Place the lid end of the canister down. Cut three triangle fins out of cardstock paper, and add them to your rocket with a piece of tape on each side. (Make sure the fins are flush with the bottom.) Cut a circle out of printer paper, and make a wedge cut from the edge to the center, so you can roll it into a cone the same diameter as your rocket. Attach the cone to the top of the rocket with tape.

Once the rockets are complete, take them outside. Turn the rockets upside down, and remove the canister lids. Tell the kids to line up in a row while you add one inch of water to each canister. Hand each kid a fizzy tablet broken in half. Tell them to quickly drop the broken tablet into the canister, replace the lid, and place their rocket on the launch platform (level sidewalk). Now, stand back, and wait until the rockets blast off!

MAKE YOUR OWN GALAXY

- Oatmeal tubs or Pringles cans
- Flashlights
- Pushpins
- Batteries

Give each child one empty oatmeal tub, or Pringles can, and a push pin. Demonstrate how to poke holes in the bottom of their containers. Now, turn the lights off in the room, and insert flashlights into the cans. If it's dark enough, you will see a ceiling and wall full of stars. Wiggle the flashlights to make them twinkle. Go the extra mile and have them poke the holes in the shapes of constellations. You can find these online.

LIGHT UP CD SPACESHIPS

- Large, plastic Easter eggs
- Silver elastic string
- Aluminum foil
- Blank CDs
- *Mini tap lights*
- Hot glue gun
- Batteries
- Star stickers (gold, blue, green)

Round, *mini tap lights* can be found in packs of three or four at the dollar store, or supercenter. Before the party, add batteries to the lights, and use a small drill bit to add a hole in the top and bottom of each plastic egg. During the party, hand each kid one-half of a plastic egg, and a 12-inch length of silver elastic string. Demonstrate how to fold the string in half, and make a double knot to form a loop, and feed the loop through the hole in the egg, so that the knot is on the inside. Give each child a piece of aluminum foil to cover the outside of an egg. Make sure the silver hoop pokes through the foil at the top. Let each of the kids decorate a blank CD with star stickers. When their finished, remove the double-stick tape on the back of the *mini tap lights*, and attach it to the center of the CD. Use the hot glue gun to attach the foil-covered egg half to the opposite side of the CD. Hang the space ships as night-lights!

CHAPTER 12

THE COMPLETE GUIDE TO A PIRATE PARTY!

Yo, Ho, Ho! It's a Pirate's life for me!
So grab your sword, and hop on board, we'll sail the Seven Seas!

PIRATE INVITES

GOLDEN COINS

A pirate is always happy to find a new treasure! Use small bags filled with gold foil chocolate coins or golden nugget bubblegum for your Invite Favors. Tie a piece of ribbon or twine around the tops to attach the Invite Tags.

GROG BOTTLES

Pick up some old-fashioned root beer in brown glass bottles. Plan a few "Root Beer Float Fridays" with the family until all of the bottles are empty. Rinse out the bottles and let them dry. Print two Invites on each piece of tan parchment so they are small enough to fit into the bottles. Plug each bottle with a cork, and tie a piece of raffia around the bottleneck.

TREASURE MAPS

Did you know that treasure maps date all the way back to 100 A.D.? For centuries, people have been keeping maps to locate their valuables, but pirates were the ones that added secret codes to keep their untrustworthy shipmates from stealing their loot! So, let's make a map that only your most honorable pirate friends can read!

Print out a regular map from school to your party. Place a piece of tracing paper over the top of it, and use a fine tip marker to trace the route with dotted lines. Make sure you turn the right angles into meandering curves, and label your landmarks with sea-worthy names; Johnson Elementary becomes "Johnson Key", a restaurant becomes "Last Meal Island"! Add whirlpools, coral reefs, sunken ships, shark fins and a few waves.

Finally, mark your destination with a hearty *X*! Now make copies of your map on tan parchment paper. Print your Invite on the reverse side using a *pirate-y* font. When you're done, roll up each invite, and tie your treasure maps closed with a piece of raffia. You can also melt a red crayon to add a thick circle of melted wax on the seam to look like a royal seal!

Here's an example of how you might word your Pirate Party Invite:

> **Ahoy there me hearties! Ye better have fear,**
> **Nicholas' birthday be drawin' near!**
> **Yer presence be demanded at a Party we planned,**
> **For only real pirates, not lubbers of land!**
> **Our ship will be sailing June 20 at NOON**
> **If yer not thar you'll be meetin' yer doom!**
> **7735 Main Street- 555-5555**

PIRATE FAVORS

Things like pirate eye patches, mini-telescopes, skull rings, bandanas, pirate hooks, toy swords, skull goblets, and stuffed parrots are easy enough to find online.

PIRATE HAT FAVORS

Order a dozen pirate hats and personalize them with pearl-colored puff paint. Use an online "Scalawag Name Translator" to convert the kids names to something *pirate-y*!

LOOT BAGS

Near the end of the party, gather some of your decorative gold coins, jewels, small favors, and leftover treats. Divide the loot into red bandanas, and tie opposite corners.

PIRATE DECORATIONS

TREASURE CHEST

Every pirate needs a place to keep his booty! Plastic and cardboard pre-made treasure chests are easy enough to find online, but if you want to get your kids in on the action, make one yourself!

- Cardboard box or Styrofoam cooler
- Brown (and gold) craft paint
- Aluminum foil & newspaper
- Glue stick
- Wooden dowel
- Jewels

Paint the box or cooler with brown craft paint. (Spray paint will melt Styrofoam.) Let it dry completely, and then use a glue stick to attach aluminum foil hinges and latches, or just paint them on with gold craft paint. Use a wooden dowel to prop open the lid, and stuff newspaper into the bottom for filler. Add a bounty of plastic gold coins, jewels, strings of pearls and beads.

PIRATE FLAGS

What respectable pirate would set sail without hoisting his Jolly Roger? **His what?** His pirate flag! Black flags with skulls and crossbones are called Jolly Rogers. Did you know that name came from the French words *joli rouge* (pretty red)? Back in the day, pirates hoisted bloody flags to strike terror in the hearts of their intended victims. Plant a bit of fear in the mind of your party guests by using some poster putty to attach a large Jolly Roger to your front door. If you have a flagpole, even better! Arrrgh!

GOLD COINS AND JEWELS

You can find plastic coins and jewels just about anywhere! Clean out your costume jewelry box. Search clearance bins for Mardi gras beads and discontinued craft jewels. Stop by a few garage sales; you might find a great pirate treasure for only a quarter!

LIFE SIZE PIRATES

Order a Design-a-Room Pirate kit online. These inexpensive, vinyl wall coverings will transform any ordinary room into a Pirate Ship! The kit comes with a life-size pirate, cannon, barrels, cannon balls, and shark fins. Cut them out and attach to your walls with tape or poster putty. I bought mine several years ago for less than fifteen dollars. I have used it repeatedly for Halloween and other parties. (The barrels work great for a Wild West theme.) After the party, carefully remove the tape and roll them up into a poster tube for easy storage.

PIRATE PENNANT BANNERS

100 feet of these awesome black pirate skull flags will *pirate-up* any room! Hang some across your front porch or use them like streamers in your Party Room. If you have extra, tape them around the edge of the snack buffet or your kitchen counter! You can also make your own pirate pennant banners with black construction paper, skull stickers, and string.

WOODEN CRATES

Looks like the pirates have raided some cargo ships! Pick up some used boxes from the grocery or a local moving company. Have your teenage helper or older kids drag the boxes into the backyard, and paint them with an old roller and a quart of brown latex paint from the hardware store. (Spray paint doesn't cover well.) They don't have to be perfect. After the boxes dry completely, stencil on words like *Property of Her Majesty, Black Pearl,* or *HMS Pinafore.* Hop on your computer and print out words in Arabic, Chinese, and French. Tape them to the crates. These pirates have been plundering across the globe! Stack the boxes in piles of two or three around the Party Room. Hang a rope or pirate hat from the corner of the stack.

TABLE COVERS

Buy some inexpensive brown broadcloth or burlap at your local fabric store. Cover the tables, leaving a 12-inch drop on all sides. Use scissors to tatter the edges by cutting strips every three inches. Cover the tablecloths with fishing nets and add sand, seashells, plastic coins, and jewels.

PIRATE FOOD

BOOTY BUFFET

Line up several glass fishbowls, and fill them with black seedless grapes (cannon balls), baby carrots (peg legs), Hershey Nuggets (gold bullion), Ring Pops, Juju cherry coins, gold wrapped coins, butterscotch candies, multi-colored cheddar goldfish, Swedish Fish and gummy sharks!

PIRATE TEETH

Pirates spend many months on the sea, far away from the dentist, so pick up a few bags of Original Corn Nuts. These crunchy corn snacks look just like gross, yellow pirate teeth!

SEA-WORTHY SAUSAGE STACKERS

Cube a log of sausage and a block of your favorite cheese. Stack one piece of cheese between two cubes of sausage, and skewer with sword-shaped toothpicks.

FRIED PARROT LEGS

Save yourself some time, and send your husband or best friend to pick up a bucket of chicken a few hours before the party. You can pre-order specific pieces in the Deli Dept. of most groceries. Set your oven to 175. Place pieces into an uncovered roasting pan until serving. (The chicken will start to dry out after two hours.)

WATERMELON SHIP

These awesome centerpieces look more difficult to make than they actually are! The night before the party, carve the top off a watermelon using a serrated knife or a pumpkin carving knife. (Use a permanent marker to draw your line before you cut.) Scoop out balls of watermelon with a melon baller. Discard the seeds. Place the melon balls into a separate bowl. Use a serving spoon to clean out the rest of the flesh and smooth the inside of the watermelon. Remove the extra flesh from the inside of the top portion, and carve it into a *main sail* (a square with two concave sides). Use an 18-inch long, ¼-inch wooden dowel as a *mast* for the sail. Fill the watermelon with seedless green and black grapes (cannonballs), strawberries, cantaloupe, honeydew, pineapple chunks, and watermelon balls. The weight of the fruit will help keep the mast erect. Insert a row of shorter dowel pieces on either side as oars. Keep your watermelon ship refrigerated until the party.

COOL IDEA!

Once you add the other fruit to the ship, you will have a ton of leftover watermelon balls. Freeze them in a gallon-size plastic zipper bag, and use them to make frozen watermelon slushies. (You won't want to eat them if they thaw, the freezing breaks down the cellular structure, and thawing turns them into grainy pulp.)

OCTOPUS SANDWICHES

Slice hot dogs down the middle with a sharp knife. Lay each half flat and slice again so you have four long *legs*. Cook in a shallow frying pan until the *legs* start to curl. Stuff the *legs* into dollar rolls making sure they hang out the sides a bit. Add some shredded lettuce and a squirt of mustard or ketchup. Serve with *coral* corn chips.

SEAWEED PASTA

Boil some spinach linguini and serve with butter and parmesan cheese, or make a few quick boxes of shells and cheese. (Add milk to loosen the stiff noodles.)

APPLE BOATS

Slice some red and green apples into wedges. Remove the seeds, and insert a pretzel stick into the center of each wedge. Add one-half slice of American cheese to the pretzel as a sail.

POLLY PINWHEELS

- Carrots
- Red peppers
- Zucchini
- Yellow squash
- Dry Ranch dip
- Cream cheese
- Sour cream
- Tortillas

The night before the party, use a large-hole box grater to shred the vegetables. Add the shredded vegetables, a brick of cream cheese, ¼ cup of sour cream, and the packet of dry Ranch dip to a gallon size plastic zipper bag. Remove the air and zip the bag closed. Mix the ingredients by smooshing the bag from the outside. When thoroughly combined, smooth a ¼-inch thick layer onto each flour tortilla. Roll the tortillas tightly, and wrap in clear plastic wrap. Refrigerate until the party. Use a sharp knife to slice the rolls into ½-inch spirals, and serve them on a platter covered with dry, green leafy lettuce. What a great way to get pirates to eat their vegetables!

PIRATE DESSERTS

CAP'N CRUNCH TREATS

- Chocolate chips
- Butterscotch chips
- Mini-marshmallows
- Cap'n Crunch Cereal

Add one cup of chocolate chips, and one cup of butterscotch chips to a large bowl. Melt the chips in the microwave. (Be careful not to over-heat. The chocolate will get crumbly.) Add 6 cups of cereal and one cup of mini-marshmallows. Mix well. Fold the mixture into a well-greased 9 x 13-cake pan. Let cool for one hour, then cover with waxed paper until the party. Turn the pan over onto a cutting board, and slice into treat-size bars with a serrated knife.

SUNKEN TREASURE CAKE

- Prepared angel food cake
- Blueberry gelatin
- Whipped topping
- Strawberries

Place the angel food cake on serving plate. Cut 3/4-inch-thick horizontal slice from top of cake using a serrated knife. With small knife, cut one-inch wide and one-inch deep tunnel inside center of cake. (Be careful not to cut through.) Set two bowls on the counter. In Bowl A, prepare the blueberry gelatin as directed on box. Remove one-half cup of gelatin and pour into Bowl B. Refrigerate Bowl A for 10 minutes. Add a tub of whipped topping to Bowl B, whisk until blended, and refrigerate. When Bowl A has thickened, stir in ¾ cups of chopped strawberries and spoon into tunnel of cake. Replace top of cake. Remove Bowl B from refrigerator and frost cake with whipped topping gelatin mixture. Garnish the top with more strawberries. Refrigerate until serving.

SANDY BEACH

In a large bowl, prepare a box of instant vanilla pudding. Whisk until blended. Let stand five minutes. Crush several vanilla wafers (saving some for decoration.) Add whipped topping and crushed wafers. Spoon into clear plastic cocktail cups, and refrigerate until the party. Top with a whole vanilla wafer before serving.

SEVEN SEAS SUNSET POPS

Easy peasy! Mix orange juice, lemon-lime soda and cranberry juice. (2-2-1 ratio) Drop Maraschino cherries into plastic pop-sicle trays. Fill with orange juice mixture, allowing for expansion. Freeze overnight. Run under warm water to release pops before serving.

PIRATE DRINKS

RUBY RED PUNCH

Make some ice cubes out of red fruit punch. Add the cubes to a punch bowl with a gallon of chilled fruit punch and one liter of lemon-lime soda.

CLASSIC PIRATE ALE

A pirate can't live without his grog! Pick up some old-fashioned root beer in brown glass bottles. (You might have some leftover from your invite project.) Orange, Strawberry, or Cream soda will work too. Ice them down in an aluminum washtub (or 35-gallon storage tote). Don't forget to recycle.

COOL IDEA!

Teach the kids how to blow across the top of their bottles to make them whistle. The bottles will have a different pitch depending on how much liquid is inside it. An empty bottle sounds a lot like blowing into a Conch shell!

PIRATE INDOOR ACTIVITIES

WALK THE PLANK

Place a long, 2 X 4 piece of wood on the floor. Blindfold the first player, spin them around a few times, and then line them up at one end of the *plank*. See how far along the plank they can walk before they fall off. Use a permanent marker to mark how far they walked. Have each kid take turns. Whichever player gets the farthest wins! If walking across is too easy, spin the pirates a few more times!

PARROT ME

Have the players sit in a circle. One player starts the game by making a body movement such as wiggling nose, clapping hands, shaking head, shrugging shoulders, etc. The next player must repeat the first player's move and add a new movement. The third player must copy the first two movements in the order they were made, and then add their own movement. Play continues around the circle. When a player can't remember all of the movements in the right order, they're out!

CANNONBALL POP

My kids love this simple activity. Inflate several black balloons. Put them in the middle of a large open carpeted area. Have the pirates stand in a circle around the balloons. When you say *go*, all of the pirates run to a balloon and try to pop it without using their hands. Stomp on it, sit on it, lay on it, or squeeze it.

UH UM ERR

One player comes up with a topic. Another player has to keep talking about that topic without saying *uh* or *um* for one minute. If they say *uh* or *um* before the time is up, they're out. The last player to stay in the game without saying *uh* or *um* is the winner!

THE CAPTAIN SAYS

Choose one player to be the captain. Have the rest of the players stand in a row. The captain gives orders to the other players to make motions. *The captain says thumbs up. The captain says hop on one foot. The captain says hands on your head.* If the captain doesn't say, *the captain says*, before an order, the players do not follow the order. Any player who makes the motion is out of the game. The winner is the player who remains in the game the longest.

BUST OPEN A PIÑATA

The night before the party, fill a piñata with wrapped candy and small toys. Toss a rope over a sturdy tree limb or a rafter in your garage. Tie one end to the piñata. Have an adult hold the other end to control the height of the piñata. Choose one child to go first. Have the other children stand back. (Use masking tape to make a line for them to stand behind, and away from the swinging stick.) Blindfold the first child and give them a stick or broom handle. Spin the child around three times and point them in the direction of the piñata. Let the child swing the stick three times. Increase the difficulty by raising or lowering the piñata as the child swings. Try to make sure each child gets a turn before allowing the piñata to be broken open.

PIRATE OUTDOOR ACTIVITIES

TREASURE DIVE

If you have a swimming pool, this is a great game! Have the pirates put on their goggles and snorkel masks, and line up along one side of the pool with their backs to the water. While they're not looking, scatter gold coins and large plastic jewels into the water. When you say *go*, the pirates turn around and dive into the water all at once. The object of the game is to see who can find the most coins and jewels. Have them each pick a spot along the edge of the pool to store their *booty* while they dive for more.

PIRATE PEG LEG RACE

Mark a starting and a finishing line with tape or string. Divide the pirates into pairs. Match them evenly by height. Tie one of each pair's ankles with a scarf or bandana. Right leg to left leg, so they're both facing the same direction. Make sure there isn't anything hanging down to trip the team and don't tie it too tight. Set up everyone at the starting line. When you say *go*, the pirates race to the finish!

SHIP WARS

The night before the party, make a basket full of *cannonballs* by crumpling pieces of newspaper into balls the size of a tennis ball. Cover the balls with strips of electrical tape so they keep their form. (Don't crumple too tightly or the balls will be too hard to throw at each other.) On the day of the party, mark two 4 x 8-foot *ships* approximately 10 feet apart. Divide the pirates into two teams and have them stand on their *ships*. Give each team an even number of *cannonballs*. Let the pirate attack begin! The object of the game is to get as many cannonballs as possible onto the enemy ship before time runs out. Pirates can throw back any cannonballs that land on their ship.

PIRATE CRAFTS

PIRATE HATS

This classic project is still a ton of fun for little ones! Take a one-half sheet of newspaper and fold it in half. Take each of the two folded corners and fold them down towards the middle making a triangle. Fold one of the bottom flaps up to form a brim. Turn the hat over and fold up the other brim. Secure the brims with a few pieces of clear tape. You can also use large sheets of black construction paper or brown paper grocery bags. Let the kids decorate their pirate hats with markers and skull stickers. When the hats are ready to wear, have the kids open up the middle, and put them on with the points over their ears. (Facing the points from front to back looks more like a sailor hat, and a pirate would never wear a sailor hat!)

SPYGLASS TELESCOPES

- Paper towel or gift-wrap tubes
- Black and yellow construction paper
- Clear tape
- Plastic wrap

Cut the tube to the length of your construction paper, and tape plastic wrap over one end of the tube. Cover the outside of the tube with black construction paper. Add a ½-inch strip of yellow paper to trim both ends. For a sturdier telescope, use black and yellow duct tape instead of construction paper.

PARROT BUDDIES

- Sticky glue dots
- Colored poms (large and small)
- Spring clothes pins
- Googly eyes
- Colored feathers
- Yellow craft foam (beak)

Bags of colored poms and feathers are available at any craft store. Red, blue, and green make great parrots! Make a parrot body by attaching a large pom to a clothespin with a glue dot. Add a small pom head to the top. Press the poms together to make sure the head sticks. Add googly eyes, a beak, and a feather on each side for wings. Clip your parrot buddy on your shoulder!

CAPTAIN HOOKS

- Black duct tape
- Pop-sicle sticks
- Aluminum foil
- 16 oz plastic cups

Give each pirate a pop-sicle stick and an 18 x 18-inch piece of foil. Have them crumple the foil around the top half of the stick, leaving enough hanging off the end to form into a flat hook shape. Add more foil if needed, and use a dictionary to flatten the hook. Make a slit in the bottom of each cup with scissors, and then cover the rest of the cup with strips of black duct tape (leaving the new hole exposed.) Slide your hook into the end of the cup so that the uncovered part of the stick can be held inside the cup as a handle. Add a few smaller pieces of tape to the bottom of the hook to keep it from sliding out of the cup. When you're finished, fill a giant bowl with mini-pretzel twists. Let the pirates compete to hook as many pretzels as they can!

CHAPTER 13

THE COMPLETE GUIDE TO A SLUMBER PARTY!

Some of the best childhood memories have something to do with a slumber Party!

SLUMBER PARTY INVITES

PERSONALIZED PJS

This is, by far, the most popular Invite Favor I've made for my own kids' parties, and only cost a few dollars to make. Pick up XXL men's colored t-shirts from the supercenter, and some broad-tipped fabric markers from the craft store. (You will find a million uses for these.) Stick to 100% cotton shirts, and wash them before personalizing. After the shirts are dry, write the girls' names across the back of the shirts. Add something fun to the front. *I survived Slumber Party 2010* or *Slumber 'til you drop*! When you're finished, roll them up, and use ribbon to attach the Invite Tags. Remind your guests to bring their cool PJs to the party, and take a group picture to include with your Thank You Notes.

PAPER FORTUNE TELLERS

Do you remember these from when we were kids? If you don't, you will, once you start folding! Cut pink, heavyweight paper (but not cardstock) into 8 ½ x 8 ½ inch squares. Follow these directions exactly. It's much easier than it sounds!

1. Fold the paper diagonally to form a triangle. Unfold and re-fold the opposite corners to form another triangle. There should be an X-shaped crease in the middle of the paper.
2. Fold the four corners to meet perfectly in the center of the X.
3. Turn the piece over, and fold the four corners to meet in the center. If you did it correctly, you will have four triangle flaps on one side, and four, square flaps on the other.
4. Turn the paper so the triangle flaps are facing up. Fold the paper in half diagonally. Unfold and fold the opposite corners.
5. Turn the paper over so the four squares are on top. If you sharpened the creases enough, the center corners of each square should stick up forming four finger pockets. Insert your thumb and index finger of each hand into the pockets.
6. Open the Fortune Teller. Use fancy or fun colored markers to write numbers on each triangle flap, and the corresponding Fortune on the underside of each flap:

ONE, TWO - We're inviting you...
THREE, FOUR - to fall asleep on the floor,
FIVE, SIX - play games and watch some flicks!
SEVEN, EIGHT - Prepare to stay up late!

7. Open the flaps and write party details in the blank middle square:

Gabriela's 10th birthday!
SLUMBER PARTY
October 13th 6 pm-10 am
7735 Main Street - RSVP 555-5555

PERSONALIZED PILLOWCASES

Pick up some inexpensive pillowcases and a package of iron-on transfer letters at the supercenter. Pre-wash the pillowcases and personalize with each girls name or initials. Roll them up and attach Invite Tags with colorful ribbon. Remind the girls to bring their pillowcases to the party!

SLUMBER PARTY FAVORS

With a Slumber Party, many of the craft activities can serve as Party Favors, but if you still feel the need to send the girls home with more, fill pairs of funny toe socks (socks that have toes) with dollar store items like: nail polish, eye shadow, lip gloss, glow bracelets, journals or bubble bath.

MAKE A PLAN!

For a regular two-hour party, I'd suggest three 20-minute activities, but a Slumber Party is a whole other ballgame! For example, if your guests arrive around 6 p.m. and stay up until 12 p.m. (standard slumber party bedtime), you'll have to plan activities for about *6 hours in the evening* and *2 hours in the morning* before pick-up. That's a total of eight party hours. Ack! Don't get overwhelmed. Remember, you'll probably spend: 30 minutes eating dinner; one hour singing happy birthday, eating cake, and opening presents; two hours watching a movie (and you should absolutely plan to watch a movie); and 30 minutes in the morning cleaning up and eating breakfast. This really leaves only **3-4 evening hours and *1-1 ½ morning hours* for planned activities- completely manageable.**

In the following sections, I've added approximately how long each activity should last. Browse and choose a mix of high and low energy activities. Reserve a few quick and easy ideas in case the girls get bored. Be flexible, and remember half the fun of having a Slumber Party is spending time with friends!

BEFORE THE PARTY

- Clear excess clutter and remove anything that might get broken during an impromptu pillow fight, or a 2 a.m. stumble to the bathroom. Push the tables, chairs, and sofas against the wall, leaving plenty of open space in the middle for sleeping bags. Add a pile of beanbags, extra pillows, and blankets in the corner.
- If there is a television, be sure the DVD player and/or Karaoke machines are connected and ready to use. Fill a basket with appropriate movies and karaoke CDs. If you don't have a karaoke machine, hook up a microphone to your CD player or stereo, (available at the supercenter for less than ten dollars).
- Add a small snack buffet. (See Recipe Section) This will prevent the girls from rummaging through the kitchen in the middle of the night.
- Fill a basket with teen magazines and flashlights in case anyone has trouble falling asleep. Load a laundry basket with games: Sorry, Clue, Yahtzee, Jenga, Uno, Dominos, and standard playing cards. Print the directions to a few card games and attach them to the deck of cards with a rubberband. (See Activities Section)
- Make sure there's extra toilet paper and fresh towels in the bathroom. (If the girls are of a certain age, make sure there are appropriate *girl supplies* under the sink. You never know.)
- String colored holiday lights or rope light around the Party Room. When it's time for everyone to settle down (or attempt to settle down), turn off the other lights.
-

DURING THE PARTY

- As the girls arrive, give each parent a short overview of what you have planned (to calm any nerves). Ask if there are any allergies, medications, or nighttime issues you need to know about. Have a spiral notebook available to write down contact information. In the event of an emergency, it's helpful to have everyone's info.

- Have the Birthday Kid lead the girls to the Party Room, and help arrange the sleeping bags in a *starburst* with pillows in the middle for late-night gossip and giggles. (This will also prevent arguments over who gets to sleep next to whom.)
- After the girls are settled, welcome them and tell them about the fun activities you have planned. This is also when you should make a clear declaration of the rules: NO prank phone calls and NO going outside (this will include TPing and Ding Dong Ditch). Set the rules for texting and computer use. If you've planned enough fun activities, these are the only rules you'll need.

SLUMBER PARTY FOOD

(Look for additional recipes in the "Fun in the Kitchen" Section.)

LATE-NIGHT NIBBLERS BUFFET

Stock a table in the Party Room with bottles of flavored water. Add a row of glass fishbowls filled with pretzel rods, dried banana chips, fruit roll-ups, candy necklaces, cookies, cheese-peanut butter crackers, and Strawberry Crunch (See Desserts Section).

PARTY PIZZAS

- 3-inch cocktail rye
- pound block of Velveeta
- pound roll of sausage
- 1 cup of ketchup

The day before the party, brown the sausage in a skillet and drain. Return to skillet and add cubed Velveeta and ketchup. Cook on low heat until Velveeta is melted. Stir frequently. Arrange cocktail bread on waxed paper. Top each slice of bread with a spoonful of Velveeta mixture. Let cool completely, and stack in a plastic gallon-size zipper bag. Freeze overnight. When you're ready to serve, preheat the oven to 325. Place the pizzas on cookie sheets. Bake 15-20 minutes or until bread is toasted. These will keep in the freezer for up to a month. When you're ready to serve, bake in a 325 degrees oven until toasted.

MOVIE NIGHT SHOE BOXES

Before the party, collect enough new or gently used shoeboxes so that each girl will have one. Cover the inside of the boxes with aluminum foil, and decorate the outside with fun stickers or markers. Add each girl's name to a box. When it's time to watch a movie, fill the boxes with popcorn, candy, and a drink box.

SNACK TRAYS

- Celery, carrot chips, and grape tomatoes with a tub of Ranch
- Grapes, strawberries and melon balls with vanilla yogurt
- Sausage and cheese cubes with goldfish crackers
- Tortilla chips and salsa
- Rye bread bowl with dill dip

SLUMBER PARTY BREAKFAST

BAGEL BUFFET

- Toaster
- Sliced bagels
- Flavored cream cheese
- Peanut butter
- Strawberry jam
- Pancake syrup
- Bananas
- Scrambled eggs
- Sausage patties
- American cheese

Toast the bagels and let the girls assemble their own sandwiches; PBJB-Peanut butter and jam bagels; PBSB-Peanut butter and syrup bagels; PBBB- Peanut Butter and banana bagels; Sausage, egg, and cheese bagels, etc.

MACGYVER BREAKFAST

Pick up a variety pack of individual mini-boxes of cereal. Open the boxes, and use scissors to cut off the tops of each plastic bag. Pour milk right into the bag inside the box; Cereal with no bowl!

HOMEMADE DONUTS

Open a few cans of refrigerated biscuits, and pre-heat one inch of vegetable oil in a large skillet. Open a few cans of refrigerated biscuits. Press your thumb into center of each biscuits to form a small hole. Carefully place them in the skillet an inch apart. Fry until golden brown, using tongs to flip. Drain on paper towel and roll in a bowl of cinnamon and sugar.

SAUSAGE TOT CASSEROLE

- 1 lb pork sausage
- 2 cups shredded cheese
- 2 cups milk
- 2 eggs
- 2 lbs frozen tater tots

Before the party, brown the sausage in a skillet and drain. Let cool and refrigerate in a plastic zipper bag. In the morning, pre-heat the oven to 350. Spread the pre-cooked sausage into the bottom of a 9x13-glass casserole. Sprinkle on the cheese. Scramble the eggs and milk in a small bowl and pour over the cheese. Add tots, and bake for 35-45 minutes.

PANCAKES ON A STICK

Check the freezer section of your grocery store for these cool cousins to the corndog; microwaveable sausage on a stick wrapped in a pancake. They even come in blueberry! Serve with pancake syrup for dipping.

MCMOM MUFFINS

Toast English muffins, and top with pre-cooked sausage patties, scrambled eggs, and American cheese.

SLUMBER PARTY DESSERTS

ICE CREAM CONE S'MORES

- Waffle cones
- Hershey Kisses
- Marshmallows

Let the girls prepare these easy treats! Place a waffle cone in a paper cup. Add two unwrapped chocolate kisses, and a regular marshmallow. Place up to four cups in the microwave at a time. Cook for 20-30 seconds. Make sure the girls watch as the marshmallows triple in size as they cook! Carefully remove from the microwave, and let cool for a minute before eating.

CLASSIC RICE CRISPY TREATS

Melt butter ½ stick of butter and 6 cups of mini-marshmallows in a large pot. Add marshmallows and stir until melted. Add 8 cups of Rice Crispies Cereal and mix with a rubber spatula. Pour mixture into a 13 x 9 greased glass casserole. Let cool and cut into squares. Experiment with different cereals like Fruity Pebbles, Cap'n Crunch, Cocoa Crispies, or Cheerios. Add different toppings like chocolate chips, mini-M&Ms, and sliced peanut butter cups.

BROWNIE PIZZA

- Chewy brownie batter
- One can of white frosting
- Red food coloring
- 6 oz block of white chocolate
- Mini-M&Ms
- Peanut butter chips

Pre-heat oven to 350, and prepare the brownie recipe as directed on the box. Pour the mixture onto a 12-inch greased pizza pan. Bake for 20-30 minutes or until a toothpick comes out clean. Let the brownie pizza cool completely. Mix red food coloring into the can of frosting until its red like pizza sauce. Use a rubber spatula to spread the *sauce* on the pizza. Shred the block of white chocolate with a box grater, and spread the *cheese* over the pizza. Add candy toppings. Use a pizza cutter to slice the brownie pizza into narrow pizza slices and serve.

CHOCOLATE CHIP ICE CREAM SANDWICHES

The day before the party, sandwich scoops of softened vanilla ice cream between chocolate chip cookies. Dunk ½ of the sandwich into a bowl of melted Hershey's chocolate. Place on waxed paper and freeze until the party.

CHOCOLATE COVERED STRAWBERRIES

- Large strawberries with hulls
- Chocolate bars or Hershey Kisses
- Cupcake liners

Gently rinse the strawberries, and let them dry completely on a stack of paper towels. Arrange cupcake liners in a plastic cake server. Use a cereal bowl to microwave a few broken chocolate bars or unwrapped Hershey Kisses, 30 seconds at a time, stirring frequently until smooth. (Be careful not to over-heat. The chocolate will get crumbly.) Gingerly gather the leaves and stem of each strawberry with the tips of your fingers, and dip them into the warm chocolate. Roll to coat on all sides. Scrape the excess chocolate off on the edge of the bowl and lay the strawberry on its side in a cupcake liner. Cover with waxed paper and refrigerate. These will last in the refrigerator for up to 48 hours before getting mushy.

STRAWBERRY CRUNCH

- 9 cups Rice Chex
- 1 ½ cups of chocolate chips
- ¼ cup of butter
- 1 tsp vanilla
- 1 ½ cups powdered sugar
- 1 box of strawberry gelatin

Add cereal to a large bowl and set aside. Microwave the chocolate chips, butter, and vanilla in an uncovered small bowl, stirring frequently. Pour the warm mixture over the cereal and blend with a rubber spatula. Mix powdered sugar and gelatin in plastic zipper bag. Sprinkle over the cereal mixture. Seal bowl with plastic wrap and shake until well coated.

RAINBOW SWIRL CAKE

- One box of vanilla cake mix
- One box of strawberry cake mix
- One box of chocolate cake mix
- One can of frosting

Mix each cake mix according to the directions in separate bowls. Spray non-stick cooking spray in a 13 X 9 X 2 glass casserole. Pour the chocolate batter in one end, the vanilla mixture in the middle, and the strawberry mixture in the other end. Gently swirl the three colors together with a spatula. Bake at 350 for 30 to 35 minutes. Let cool and frost.

SLUMBER PARTY DRINKS

SHIRLEY TEMPLES

These are a fun blast from the past! Add grenadine or pomegranate juice to plastic cocktail cups of lemon-lime soda. Top with maraschino cherries.

PINK LEMONADE

Mix a batch of frozen pink lemonade and add slices of fresh lemons to the pitcher.

SLUMBER PARTY PUNCH

- Orange juice
- Cranberry juice
- Lemon-lime soda
- Oranges
- Maraschino cherries

The day before the party, make an ice ring by adding orange slices and a jar of cherries to the bottom of a small, round, plastic chip server, (the kind with space in the middle for dip). Cover the oranges and cherries with cranberry juice and freeze overnight. As the girls arrive, pour orange juice, lemon-lime soda and cranberry juice (2-2-1 ratio) into a punch bowl. Run warm water over the bottom of the ice ring to release from the plastic, and add it to the punch.

TWINKIE SHAKES

- Two cups milk
- Six Twinkies
- Four Oreo cookies
- Three cups of vanilla ice cream

Add all ingredients to a blender. Blend until smooth.

FUN IN THE KITCHEN!

Here are some great recipes the girls can make on their own, or with a little supervision. Order some fun, paper chef hats for less than five dollars online. The girls will love wearing them while they create their masterpieces.

PIGS IN A BLANKET

Open two cans of refrigerated biscuits. Cut hot dogs in half and wrap in the biscuits. Place on a cookie sheet. Bake as directed on the can.

BISCUIT PIZZAS

Open two cans of refrigerated biscuits. Flatten the biscuits, and place them in a muffin pan. Add spaghetti sauce, shredded mozzarella and diced pepperoni or pre-cooked sausage. Bake as directed.

VEGGIE PIZZA

Pre-heat the oven to 375. Open two cans of refrigerated crescent rolls, and press the rectangles into a cookie sheet. Bake 13-15 minutes. Supervise the girls as they shred carrots, dice raw broccoli and cauliflower, and cube cucumbers and tomatoes. (If the girls are too young to work with knives, prepare the veggies before the party and store in plastic zipper bags.) Let baked crescent crust cool for 15 minutes. In a bowl, mix a softened brick of cream cheese with an envelope of dry ranch dressing mix. Use a rubber spatula to spread mixture onto the crust, and top with veggies.

OVEN PIES

Open two cans of refrigerated biscuits. Flatten the biscuits. Add a tablespoon of any flavor pie filling. Fold in half and seal the edges with the tines of a fork. Bake as directed. Sprinkle with powdered sugar.

BACON TRIANGLES

Pre-heat the oven to 375. Open two cans of refrigerated crescent rolls, and separate each into eight rectangles. Press the perforations together to seal each rectangle. Use a pizza cutter to cut each rectangle into four squares. Add a heaping teaspoon of real bacon bits, and a tsp of shredded cheese to each square. Fold the squares in half forming filled triangles. Press the edges together to seal. Place the triangles on cookie sheets. Beat a raw egg and use a pastry brush to coat the top of each triangle. Sprinkle parmesan cheese on each. Bake 9-11 minutes.

STRAWBERRY ROLL UPS

Pre-heat the oven to 350. Unroll two cans of crescents, and separate into 16 triangles. Unwrap eight strawberry fruit roll ups, and cut diagonally in half. Add a triangle of fruit roll up to each crescent, and start with the wide end to roll them. Place the crescents on a non-stick cookie sheet. Bake for 12-15 minutes. In a small bowl, mix 1 cup powdered sugar and 1/3 cup of milk to a glaze consistency. Drizzle over warm crescents.

COOL WHIP COOKIES

Pre-heat the oven to 350. In a bowl, combine one box of cake mix (any flavor), one tub of whipped topping, and two eggs. Mix thoroughly with a sturdy metal spoon. (The dough will be thick and sticky.) Drop walnut-sized dough balls into a bowl of powdered sugar. Coat completely, and place on a non-stick cookie sheet. Bake for 15 minutes. As the cookies expand, the powdered sugar coating will crack and expose the dough color. Try several cake mix flavors like red velvet, confetti, lemon, banana, cherry chip, and of course, chocolate.

ARMPIT FUDGE
Yep, that's what it's called!

- Powdered sugar
- Cocoa powder
- Butter
- Cream cheese

Let the girls fill quart-sized plastic zipper bags with ½ cup powdered sugar, 2 tsp of cocoa powder 1 T butter and 2 tsp of cream cheese. Squeeze out the air and zip closed. Show the girls how to warm the bags under their arms, and squish them until all the ingredients are mixed well. Add things like raisins, peanut butter chips, chopped nuts or mini-M&Ms, and eat right out of the bags with spoons!

AIR POPPER POPCORN
Microwave popcorn is expensive, and often too greasy and too salty. With a hot air popper (under 15 dollars at the supercenter), you can save money and customize your toppings. Plus, kids love to watch it pop! Make a topping buffet so the girls can experiment with different flavors:

- Garlic Salt
- Chili powder
- Parmesan cheese
- Cinnamon
- Hot chocolate powder
- Strawberry milk powder
- Dry Ranch dressing
- Dry Italian dressing
- Brown sugar
- Mac n' cheese, powdered cheese
- Honey
- Chocolate syrup
- Pancake syrup
- Butter

COOL IDEA!
Since air popper popcorn doesn't have oil, butter, or salt, it's perfect for a popcorn fight!

PBJ COOKIES

Pre-heat the oven to 325. In a bowl, combine one cup of peanut butter, 1/2 cup sugar and one egg. Refrigerate for 30 minutes and roll into 18 balls. Place on a non-stick cookie sheet. Use a melon baller to make a dent in each dough ball, and add a spoonful of grape or strawberry jam. Bake for 18 minutes or until golden brown.

FONDUE DIPPABLES

Melt milk-chocolate chocolate chips in a snack-size Crock-Pot or fondue pot. Try dipping something new like rippled potato chips or crispy bacon (yes, I said bacon!) Here are some other great dippables:

- Cubed pound cake
- Strawberries
- Banana chunks
- Apple wedges
- Pretzel rods
- Graham crackers
- Marshmallows
- Vanilla wafers

SLUMBER PARTY ACTIVITIES

THE WORST MAKEOVERS EVER (30 mins)

(Over age 8) Set up a Makeover Station with inexpensive, obnoxious-colored eye shadows, lipsticks, blush, eyeliner, hair mousse, barrettes, pony holders, scarves, brushes, etc. Divide the girls into teams of three, (a make-up artist, a hair stylist, and a victim). Let the teams go to town! Be a cool mom and give helpful tips along the way. When the makeovers are finished take a vote to decide who has the worst makeover ever! Make sure you have a digital or video camera handy. To return the girls to their natural beauty, you can use tear-free baby shampoo or hypoallergenic, make-up remover towelettes.

MUMMIFIED FRIENDS (30 mins)

Divide the group into teams of three. Hand each group one roll of plain label toilet paper. When you say *go*, two players on each team have to wrap their teammate from head to toe with the toilet paper. Any torn pieces have to be picked up and tucked in somewhere. The first team to run out of toilet paper wins!

CRAZY FASHION SHOW (30-45 mins)

My girls love this activity and always ask to play it over and over! The week before the party, start gathering the craziest clothes you can find; dig through your closets, holiday boxes, and storage room. Fill one black trash bag with silly clothes; Halloween costumes, rubber boots, neon hunting clothes, funny slippers, crazy boxer shorts, aprons, hospital scrubs, (and those ugly Hawaiian shirts that hubby won't let you throw away!) Fill a second black trash bag with funny hats, reindeer antlers, scarves, Santa hats, Halloween masks, sunglasses, bunny ears, wigs, etc. If you're not sure, toss it in the bag! Have enough items so that each player has one thing to wear, and one thing to put on their head.

During the party, have the players sit in a circle. Play a game of hot potato with a stuffed animal; passing it around the circle while music plays. When the music stops, whoever has the stuffed animal, must reach into the bag without looking, and put on whatever is pulled out. Play continues until everyone has something crazy on. Start the game over to empty the second bag until all the players have something crazy on their head.

Now send the girls into the other room with whatever is leftover in the bags to finish accessorizing. Play the music, and have them come back in the room one by one, to model their new threads! Take plenty of individual pictures or video, and be sure to get a group shot to include with your Thank You Notes!

KARAOKE (60 mins)

My girls love to sing! Karaoke CDs with lyrics are available online and at the supercenter. If you don't have a karaoke machine, plug an inexpensive microphone into your CD player or stereo. You can find the lyrics to most songs on the Internet. Print them out and let the girls go to town! If you really want to make it fun, connect two or three microphones at one time! (Setting this up and making sure it works is a perfect project for hubby!)

DOTTED NAIL ART (30-45 mins)

You don't have to be a trained professional to make pretty nails!

- Craft paint (red, orange, yellow, green, blue, purple, black, brown, and white)
- Toothpicks
- Clear nail polish
- Paper cake plates
- Nail files
- Paper towels

Place all of the supplies on the table. After the girls wash and dry their hands, have them sit at the table with a partner. Show them how to shape their nails with a file. Add a dab of each color to the paper plates. Demonstrate how to use the tip of a toothpick to make dots. Dip the toothpicks in the paint to form a tiny drop. Hold the toothpick upright to add each dot. Drag the tip of the toothpick to make teardrop shapes. Arrange the tiny dots into stripes, rainbows, zigzags, etc. Practice on a paper towel. If you make a mistake, wipe it off and start over. When everyone's nails are decorated and dry, add a coat of clear polish to make the designs last. Here are some other easy designs:

- **HEARTS**- Two red dots on top of one red teardrop
- **PALM TREES**- Stack dots for a trunk and add three green teardrop branches
- **DAISIES**- One yellow dot surrounded by five white dots

FACIALS AND PEDICURES (30-45 mins)

Girls from 7-17 love this activity! Pick up a few tubes of inexpensive, clay facial mask at the supercenter. (Be sure to check with parents about skin allergies.) Tell the girls to line up their pillows on the floor next to each other, and cover them with towels. Once everyone has their hair pulled back in a pony or headband, have the girls line up so you can apply their facemasks (cheeks, nose, chin and forehead). Keep it away from their eyes and eyelids in case they forget and rub or scratch. Most clay facemasks can be left on for up to an hour. The girls will get a kick out of how strange it feels as the clay starts to dry.

When everyone has their mask on, tell them to lie down on their backs next to each other. Give each girl two cucumber slices to cover their eyes. While they lay there giggling and wait for their masks to dry, pull off their socks and paint the assembly line of toenails a crazy bright color with quick dry polish. When the masks are dry, give each girl a separate washcloth, and run warm water in the kitchen sink. You might have to supervise to help remove any leftover clay.

MORE ACTIVITIES TO CONSIDER (30-60 mins)

Charades, Pictionary, and Hot Potato are reliable party games. Try to avoid Truth or Dare games, as they can cause embarrassment or lead to mischief.

SCAVENGER HUNTS AT THE NEIGHBORS

If you live in an area with friendly neighbors close by, this is a fun easy activity for the girls. Let five or six neighbors know to expect a few visitors the evening of the party. Split the group into two teams. Give each team a paper bag, a list, and a pen. Start the game before it gets dark. If the girls are under age 10, have an adult or teenage helper tag along with each group. Send one team one way and the other team in the opposite direction. The team that returns either first, or with the most items on their list, wins! (See Chapter 14 for a Neighborhood Scavenger Hunt list.)

CARD GAMES

FOUR SCORE

The dealer gives each player four cards, facing down. The dealer gives a fifth card to the player on the left. That player quickly picks one card from their hand and passes it, face down, to the player on the left, and so on. All players keep four cards in hand at all times. The person to the right of the dealer discards one card into a pile. The dealer shuffles this pile when he runs out of cards. Continue until one person has four cards of a kind (four sevens, four jacks, etc.) That player lays his cards on the table and scores. Carry on with the remaining players. The last player who hasn't scored loses.

I DOUBT IT

Divide the deck evenly between the players. Players take turns discarding cards, face down into a center pile. The first player must discard all Aces. The second player discards twos. The third person discards threes, etc. As a player discards, they must call out the rank of the cards. Since the cards are face down, you don't have to discard the correct rank. If it's your turn to discard nines, you can actually discard any card or mixture of cards. Any player who suspects that the card(s) discarded do not match the rank you called, can challenge by saying, *I doubt it*! The cards are flipped over. If the cards match, the rank you called out, the challenger must pick up the whole discard pile and add it to their hand. If the cards do not match the rank you called out, you have to pick up the whole pile and add it to your hand. Play continues with the next rank in order. The first to get rid of all their cards wins!

CRAZY EIGHTS

The dealer gives each player seven cards, places the rest of the deck face down, and turns over the top card. The player to the left of the dealer picks one card from their hand that matches the suit or rank of the top card, and lays it on top.

If the player doesn't have a match, he takes cards from the top of the deck until he gets one. Play continues around the table with players matching the top discard or taking cards from the deck. A player may choose to pick a card from the deck even if he has a playable card, in order to change the suit to one he thinks the other players don't have, forcing them to add cards to their hand. Eights can be used to match any rank or suit and change the suit or rank to something new. The first player to run out of cards wins.

SLAPJACK

Divide the deck evenly between the players. No one can peek as the cards are dealt. Everyone holds the cards face down and takes turn adding their top card to a center pile waiting until the last second to turn it over. When someone plays a jack, the first player to slap it, wins the whole pile, and adds them to the bottom of their deck. Play continues starting with the person to the left of the *slapper*. If several people slap, the person whose hand is on the bottom wins the cards. If a player slaps a card that's not a jack, they have to give their top card to the person who played the card and they add it to the bottom of their deck. If you run out of cards, you cannot add to the pile, but can continue trying to slap a jack. If you slap something that is not a jack, you are out of the game. The player who slaps all the jacks wins!

SLUMBER PARTY CRAFTS

GRAFFITI SHORTS (30 mins)

Ask each girl to bring a pair of light-colored cotton shorts, or cut-off sweats to the party. (If they bring their own, you don't have to worry about sizes.) Set a container full of fabric markers in the middle of the table and let the girls go to town! Pass the shorts around the table to get autographs. Fill in all of the blank spaces on front and back with doodles, hearts, diamonds, clovers, daisies, squares, triangles, peace signs, stick people, stars, moons, smiley faces, school or mascot names, and text message abbreviations like BFF, LOL, and OMG! Follow the directions on the fabric markers package for finishing and care instructions.

FRIENDSHIP PINS (30 mins)

All you need is a box of safety pins and a bag of colorful seed beads from the craft store. Use paper plates to keep track of the beads as you add them to the needle side of a safety pin. Choose colorful combinations. Attach to the bottom rung of shoelace on the tops of their tennis shoes. These are so much fun to trade!

STAINED GLASS TEA LIGHTS (30 mins)

- Clear glass votive holders
- Multi-colored tissue paper
- White glue
- Battery tea light candles
- Paintbrushes
- Paper plates

Before the party, pick up some square or round, clear, smooth glass votive holders, colored tissue paper, and a package of cheap paintbrushes from the dollar store. Cut the tissue paper stacks into smaller, more manageable sheets. During the party, cover the table with newspaper, and add white glue to a few bowls. Place the stack of tissue paper in the middle, and gather the girls around the table. Hand each a glass votive and a paintbrush. Demonstrate how to paint a section on the outside of the votive with white glue, and add small torn pieces of tissue. Cover all sides (not the inside) by overlapping and layering dark and light colored tissue. Be sure to saturate the pieces to prevent bubbles and dry spots. Use the paintbrush and a dab of glue to smooth down the edges. When the votives are covered, turn them upside down on the paper plate, and use the paintbrushes to add a final layer of white glue to the outside. Add battery tea light candles to illuminate the colors from the inside. This technique can be used to make all sorts of cool stuff like drinking glass pencil holders, clear bowl candy dishes, salad plate key keepers, plastic container jewelry boxes, and baby food jars to hold cotton swabs.

FLEECE FRINGE PILLOWS (30 mins)

Easy Peasy! These are great to make while watching a movie. Before the party, pick up a few bags of pillow stuffing, and a few yards of colorful fleece at the fabric store: hot pink, daisy print, girly plaids, etc. When you get home, use sharp scissors to cut the fleece into 18-inch squares, two per guest. To make it easier, make an 18x18-inch template from cardboard, (or use an 18x18-inch ceramic tile). Place the template on top of the stack and trace around it, cutting through the layers with a utility razor knife. Fleece is stretchy, so they cuts don't have to be perfect. After you have two squares per guest, lay a ruler out about four inches from the edge and clip every two inches. Be sure to start and end two inches from each side.

During the party, let the girls pick out two squares. Demonstrate how to start in one corner, and tie corresponding pieces of fleece together (in a double knot) all the way around the pillow. Stop on the fourth side and add pillow stuffing. Continue tying double knots to finish. Use a different color or pattern on each side of the pillow. Buy several patterns and let the girls choose their own combination.

TIE-DYE SOCKS (15-30 mins)

This classic craft is so easy! There are a ton of tying and dying methods. Check the Internet for more elaborate instructions and projects. I like using this quick and simple method, so the girls have time for other crafts and games (and I have less mess to clean up). Grab a few packages of men's 100% cotton socks, and a few boxes of Rit fabric dye at the supercenter. Show the girls how to add rubber bands to small sections of the socks. Soak the socks in a very hot dye bath in your sink or a bucket as directed on the package. (If you have a double-sided stainless sink, use two colors!) Rinse with cool water until the water runs clear. Pop in the dryer.

LEARN TO FINGER WEAVE (30-90 mins)

Weave one yard to make a belt. Weave a few yards and make a plant hanger. Weave just because it's fun! All you need is one skein of multi-colored acrylic yarn for each girl. (If you choose not to wind the skeins into balls, make sure you start with the end that's tucked in the middle.)

1. Tie a loose loop around your thumb. Use your other hand to weave the yarn in this pattern: inside of index finger, outside of middle finger, inside of ring finger, outside of pinkie. Around pinkie to outside of ring finger, inside of middle finger, outside of index finger and around your palm. You should have yarn on either side of each finger, and a long strand across your palm.
2. With your palm facing up, lay the long strand above the row woven between your fingers.
3. Start with your index finger, pull the loop up and over the strand and your fingertip, so that the loop is now on the back of your finger and the long strand is *trapped* by the loops between your fingers. Repeat this step with your middle finger, ring finger, and pinkie.
4. Wrap the long strand around the back of your hand, to the palm, and above the row of loops again.
5. Repeat steps three and four.

A woven mess will start to form on the back of your hand. Don't panic! After five or six courses of wrapping and looping, the rope will start to take shape. If the loops start to bunch up between your fingers, gently grasp the beginning of your weaving and tug toward your elbow. This will even out the slipknots and make them uniform. Experiment with how loosely or tightly you pull the loops. Again, you are making a series of slipknots, if it gets too tight, tug on the loops to feed more yarn into the weaving. When you're finished, cut the yarns about six inches from the last loop. Weave the end pieces in and out of each finger loop, and tie a knot.

SALT DOUGH FUN! (45 mins, plus 30 mins.)

BASIC RECIPE

- 2 cups table salt
- 2 cups flour
- 1 cup water

ADDITIONAL SUPPLIES:

- Waxed paper & Dixie cups
- Toothpicks
- Paint brushes & paint (see below)
- Googly eyes
- Hot glue gun
- Permanent markers
- Magnets
- Large safety pins
- Clear acrylic spray
- Cookie cutters

In a large bowl, mix the salt into the water, and add the flour. Knead until the dough is smooth. If the dough is too dry, add a bit of water. If it's sticky, add a bit of flour. Give each girl a chunk of dough, a piece of waxed paper, a small pile of flour, and a Dixie cup with water. Use cookie cutters to make letters, stars, hearts, etc, or demonstrate how to roll the dough between their palms to make shapes.

- **CATERPILLAR**- Five marble-sized balls stuck together
- **LADYBUG**- One big and one little ball stuck together
- **DAISY**- A small ball surrounded by five flattened ovals

Make pieces stick together by adding a dab of water. Use toothpicks to make details like eyes and mouths. Make sure the edges are smooth and the thicknesses are even to prevent jagged edges. Place the creations on a cookie sheet and bake at 250 for an hour or so, until they are hard, and dry to the touch. Let cool for 15 minutes on a wire rack. Decorate with permanent markers or craft paint, and let dry. (Note: the new *washable* paints do not work due to the salt content in the dough.) After the girls go to sleep, put the painted projects in a cardboard box, and cover with a thin coat of clear acrylic spray. Let dry overnight. In the morning, add magnets, safety pins, and googly eyes with a hot glue gun.

RIBBON WEAVE BARRETTES (30 mins)

Do you remember making these when you were a kid? I had them in every color to match every outfit. Apparently, I was very cool back then! (At least, I thought I was.)

- Several different color spools of 1/8-inch satin ribbon
- Several 2¼-inch "Double Bar Statite" barrettes

Goody Brand has made these barrettes since the 60's. They usually come on a card of three pairs (gold, silver, and brown). Both, the ribbon and the barrettes are readily available at most supercenters. When the girls are around, demonstrate the following:

1. Cut two 1-yard lengths of ribbon. (For these instructions, we'll use one red and one blue.)
2. Thread the two lengths of ribbon through the hinge end of the barrette, so that exactly half of each color is sticking out of each side.
3. Cross the BLUE ribbon from the left side over the LEFT bar, down through the center, and under the RIGHT bar.
4. Cross the BLUE ribbon on the right side; over the RIGHT bar, down through the center and under the LEFT bar.
5. Repeat steps three and four with the RED ribbons. Continue alternating BLUE and RED.

As you weave, make sure the ribbons lie flat. Pull tightly and push the layers up toward the beginning. When you get to the bottom, weave the last ribbon so the streamers are all on one side. Tie a knot to secure!

COOL TIPS!

For shorter hair, use shorter ribbons. Add pony beads or fun crystal beads to the bottom of the streamers. This is a great project to do while watching a movie!

FUNKY FLIP FLOPS (30 mins)

Pick up some inexpensive flip-flops from the supercenter or Old Navy. Dig through clearance racks at the fabric store for several discounted spools of ribbon. Before the party, cut the ribbon into 6-inch pieces and store them in plastic zipper bags. During the party, demonstrate how to tie the ribbon pieces in double knots around the flip-flop straps, so that the tails are pointing up. Each side should hold 12 pieces of ribbon (24 per flip-flop, 48 per pair).

230

CHAPTER 14

THE COMPLETE GUIDE TO SCAVENGER HUNTS

Whether at home or around town, scavenger hunts can be a fun addition or alternative to birthday parties at home! All you need is paper, pencils, and plenty of help to supervise!

UNDER 8

Kids under age eight are a bit too young for a real scavenger hunt. Instead, fill plastic Easter eggs with theme-related treats. Hide the eggs in the yard or around the Party Room. To make it more challenging, decorate the eggs with markers or stickers, and make a list of certain colors or patterns to find. Divide the group into teams of two, and give each team a plastic grocery bag. If the teams find an egg that's not on their list, or is already in their bag, they must leave it in place. At the end of the hunt, let the teams divide the treats inside the eggs. Here's a sample list to get you started:

One golden egg

Two blue eggs

Three pink eggs

Four yellow eggs

One pink and purple egg

Two eggs with stickers

Three eggs with stripes

Four eggs with polka dots

RULES OF THUMB FOR OLDER CHILDREN: AGE 8 TO 11

Divide the kids into teams of four, and make sure there is an adult chaperone for each team.

OVER 12

These kids don't necessarily need an adult for each team, so long as they stay together, and keep a cell phone with them at all times.

NEIGHBORHOOD SCAVENGER HUNTS (60 mins)

Tell five or six friendly neighbors to expect visitors the evening of the party. Split the group into two teams. Start the game before it gets dark. Send one team one way and the other team in the opposite direction. The team that returns either first, or with the most items on their list, wins! Here's a Neighborhood Scavenger Hunt list to get you started:

Aluminum foil ball	Ketchup packet	Ribbon or bow
Band-aid	Marble	Rubberband
Brown lunch bag	Napkin	Safety pin
Business card	Old CD	Sock with a hole
Cheese slice	Paper clip	Staple
Clothespin	Paper towel	Straw
Cotton swab	Pencil	String
Dryer sheet	Pickle in a plastic bag	Tea bag
Empty water bottle	Picture of a dog	Toilet paper roll
Envelope	Piece of candy	Toothpick
Expired coupon	Pink crayon	Trash bag
Gift bag	Plastic spoon	Watch battery
Grocery receipt	Post-it note	Word search puzzle
Hotel soap	Potato	Yarn
Junk mail	Ramen noodles	Ziploc bag

MALL SCAVENGER HUNTS

These can be a blast so long as the players remember their manners. Some malls do not allow scavenger hunts, so be sure to call ahead. Set up a *home base* as a starting and finishing location. Divide the kids into two teams. Have each team set a stopwatch or alarm on their mobile phone to keep track of time. Each team should find as many items on their list before time is up. Before you start, make sure everyone understands the rules.

- No running, yelling or screaming. Be polite.
- Team must stay together at all times. No going outside.
- The designated meeting time is non-negotiable.

CLASSIC MALL SCAVENGER HUNTS (60-90 mins)

- Blue thread or string
- Box
- Brochure
- Business card
- Calendar
- Catalog
- Clearance sticker
- Clothing hanger
- Company letterhead
- Credit card application
- Disposable coffee cup
- Disposable toilet cover
- Employment application
- Empty game case
- Food sample
- French fry
- Gift box
- Gift card envelope
- Glitter
- Hanger
- Ketchup packet
- Loose bead or sequin
- Loose button
- Mall map
- Men's cologne sample
- Nametag
- Old receipt
- Paper bag with handles
- Paper clip
- Pen or pencil
- Piece of tape
- Price sticker or price tag
- Printed wedding registry
- Red marker
- Restaurant menu
- Restaurant napkin
- Shopping bag
- Staple
- Stranger's autograph
- Straw
- Sugar packet
- Tissue paper
- Wrapping paper

MALL SCAVENGER HUNTS WITH A CAMERA (1-2 hours)

Each team will need a digital camera to take pictures of at least one teammate accomplishing each task. The team that has the most photos when time is up wins!

- Asking for an application
- Asking someone for the time
- Covered in stuffed animals
- Doing the *wave*
- Eating a food sample
- Giving ketchup to a stranger
- Giving play dolls piggyback rides
- Hiding behind a tree in the mall
- Holding crazy earrings by ears
- Holding hands while walking
- Holding helium balloons
- Lying on a bench
- Looking in a mirror
- Opening the door for two people
- Pointing at a mall information map
- Pushing a baby stroller
- Reading a book
- Riding something motorized
- Riding the elevator
- Riding the escalator
- Sitting at a booth in a restaurant
- Spelling YMCA with a stranger
- Trying on an orange necktie
- Trying on very large men's shoes
- Walking up the stairs backwards
- Washing hands in a bathroom
- Wearing a hat
- Wearing a tiara
- Wearing blue eye shadow
- Wearing cowboy hats
- Wearing one high heel red shoe
- Wearing sunglasses
- With a salesman named Bill
- With someone selling food
- With someone in a jogging suit
- With someone wearing pink
- With someone with a long beard
- With someone with gray hair

THRIFTY MALL SCAVENGER HUNTS (30 mins)

Give each team five dollars and have them find as many items as they can. The team that brings back the most items wins! The teams are only allowed to purchase one of each item. They must have a receipt for each item, and no item can be free!

PARK SCAVENGER HUNTS (60 mins)

You will need two digital cameras for this scavenger hunt. Set up a *home base*. Make sure it is easy to see or find from all areas of the park. Divide the kids into two teams. Have each team set a stopwatch or alarm on their mobile phone to keep track of time. Each team should follow their list, and take one picture of each item they locate. Before you start, make sure everyone understands the rules:

- Do not leave the park (or designated search area) or talk to strangers
- Use caution when crossing the park roads
- Stay out of the woods and together at all times

Here's a Park Scavenger Hunt list to get you started:

A flower	Pine tree
Candy wrapper	Popsicle stick
Crosswalk	Sap from a tree or plant
Feather	Snail
Hugging a tree	Something plastic
In front of a convertible	Something red
Leaf with insect holes	Something shiny
Leaves from three trees	Speed bump
On the monkey bars	Stop sign
On the swings	Take-out menu
Out-of-state license plate	White fence
Piece of newspaper	Worm
Piece of wood	Yield sign

COOL IDEA!

Make a day of it! Pack a picnic lunch for everyone, and remember to bring plenty of drinks. Browse through the Activities Section of each party theme, and look for games that are appropriate to play in the park: relay races, kickball, Red Rover, etc.

RAINY DAY MAGAZINE SCAVENGER HUNTS (30 mins)

This hunt is appropriate for almost any age! All you need is a stack of old magazines, and several pair of scissors. Give each kid three or four magazines, and set a timer. When time is up, whoever has the most photos on the list wins!

Here's a sample list to get you started:

- Airplane
- Baby
- Bird
- Blue car
- Can of soda pop
- Car insurance ad
- Cartoon
- Chocolate dessert
- Clock
- Farm animal
- Funny hairstyle
- Glasses
- Ice
- Lipstick
- Nose ring
- Phone number
- Politician
- Red necktie
- Red-haired woman
- Ring
- Sunglasses
- Tennis shoe
- TV
- Toes
- Utensil
- Underwear
- Vegetable
- Water

CHAPTER 15

RANDOM COOL PARTY TIPS

- The title says it all. The following few pages contain random party tips that are important enough to mention, but never quite found a home in the rest of the book.

- If you're serving drinks in paper or plastic cups, keep a permanent marker near the stack of cups. Use it to write their name on the cup before you fill it. This will cut down on wasted cups, and prevent germ sharing. I usually tie a string to the marker cap, and hang it on the cabinet knob above the drink station or punch bowl.

- If parents are dropping off their kid for the party, keep a spiral notebook near the front door. Use it to jot down their contact numbers. In the unlikely event of an emergency, it will be handy to have everyone's numbers in the same place.

- Speaking of emergencies, take a quick inventory of your first aid kit. Make sure you have band-aids, antiseptic wipes, tweezers (for splinters), chewable antacids (for upset tummies), children's Tylenol (for headaches), and children's antihistamines (for bee stings). Be sure you have a parents permission before administering any medicine to a child that is not your own.

- If parents are staying for the party, be sure to serve a few adult snacks (veggies and dip, sub sandwich, etc.) and have adult beverages available (diet soda, iced tea, etc.)

- If your fishbowl buffet is filled with individually wrapped candy and treats, have your teenage helper or husband, divide the leftover treats into the favor bags (or plastic zipper bags) near the end of the party. This will save you money before the party and calories after the party!

- Always think twice before serving caffeinated drinks to kids. The last thing you want is a bunch of 8-year-olds bouncing off the walls (and they will)! Stick to lemonade, flavored drink mixes, and non-caffeinated soda.

- When planning party games, make sure everyone has a chance to win something, at least once, during the party.

- Make sure you involve the Birthday Kid in the planning process. If you decide to open gifts during the party, make sure to quietly, remind the Birthday Kid to be gracious, act excited, and say thank you, even if they already have one just like it.

- Don't plan the party to end at 5:00 pm, if you have to be at soccer practice by 5:30 pm. Be smart and either pick a day that has no other scheduled activities or delegate soccer practice to your husband.

EASY PEASY INDEX

INVITES

Aliens- 173
Badges & Bandanas - 15
Barf Bags- 35
Cactus Seeds- 90
Freeze Dried Ice Cream- 173
Golden Coin- 191
Grog Bottle- 191
Homemade Maracas- 89
Inconspicuous Brown Bags- 36
Invisible Ink- 106
Jars of Toxic Waste- 35
Jiffy Pop Popper- 68
Lost Slipper- 143
Magnifying Glass- 106
Mini Sombreros- 90
Moon Rocks- 173
Ocean Globe- 51
Paper Fortune Tellers- 206
Personalized Pillow Case- 207
Personalized PJs- 205
Real Coconuts- 125, 158
Real Horseshoes - 15
Royal Invites- 144
Safari Pals- 157
Sending Out an SOS- 52, 126
Slimy Test Tubes- 106
Smores Mix- 68
Something Fishy- 51
Tickets Please- 126
Toy Jeep- 157
Treasure Maps- 192
Wanted Posters - 16

FAVORS

Alien Scanning Devices- 175
Camp Shirts- 69-70
Glow in the Dark Favors- 174
Grass Skirts- 126
ID Badges- 174
Lab Coats- 107
Loot Bags- 193
Mexican Jumping Beans- 91
Moo Mixers- 17
Real Cactus Eggs- 91
Real Fish- 52
Six Packs- 17
Space Suits- 175
Weenie Roasters- 70

DECORATIONS

Bales of Straw- 17
Bandanas - 17
Blacklights- 108, 176
Bubbles- 54
Build a Campfire- 74, 163
Burlap Bags- 18
Campfire- 21, 72, 161
Cardboard Planets- 175
Citronella Candles- 129
Coral Reef-53
Dirty Under Things- 37
Dry Ice- 109
Fake Blood- 38
Floating Flowers- 128
Flower Garland- 127
Follow the Paw Prints- 159
Giant Used Cotton Swabs- 38
Gross Gauze- 37
Hazard Signs- 109
Helium Balloons- 53
Homemade Limbo- 136
Homemade Tent- 71
Instant Cacti- 21
Metallic Twist Ribbon- 177
Mexican Streamers- 92
Microscopes- 108
Mosquito Netting- 159
Outdoor Jungle Safari- 161
Painted Signs- 19, 73
Paper Mache Planets- 177

Paper Vines- 160
Pirate Flags- 194
Planetary Solar System- 176
Plastic Poo & Vomit- 37
Poker Chips & Cards- 20
Pudding Balloons- 38
Raffia Door Curtains- 128
Real Coconuts-128
Rubber Roaches & Bugs- 37
Serapes- 92
Set a Royal Table- 146
Sombreros- 91
Spider Webs- 38
Store Bought Tent- 73
Streamer Canopy- 145
Streamers- 53
Surgical Gloves- 108
Tarzan Swings- 160
Terra Cotta Pots- 92
Tiki Torches- 127, 160
Tissue Flowers- 91
Treasure Chest- 54, 193
Tumbleweeds- 19
Twinkling Stars- 176
Welcome to the Jungle- 127, 159
Wanted Posters- 18
Wild West Street Signs- 19
Wooden Crates- 18, 195
Wooden Sawhorses- 18

FOOD

Alien Nachos- 181
Ants on a Log- 74
Apple Boats- 197
Bacon Triangles- 216
Barf Dip- 40
BBQ Burgers- 23
BBQ Chicken Burritos- 94
BBQ Fingers- 40
Berry Grahams- 147
Biscuit Pizza- 215
Caterpillar Cocoons- 39
Cheesy Mice- 39
Chicken Kabobs- 130
Clam Sandwiches- 56
Corn Bread Muffins- 22
Corn on the Cob- 24, 74
Cosmic Pinwheels- 180
Elephant Sandwiches- 163
Festive Veggie Tray- 96
Fiesta Fruit- 94
Fire Ants on a Log- 163
Fish Bowl Buffet- 39
Fried Parrot Legs- 196
Frozen Eyeballs- 40
Fruit Skewers- 130
General Store- 22
Goldfish Guts- 41
Gravity Defying Bacon Bowls- 110, 179
Hawaiian Pizza- 131
Hawaiian Trail Mix- 131
Hobo Popcorn- 74
Homemade Donuts- 76, 211
Homemade Fruit Roll Ups- 74
Island Bagel Pizza- 131

Jungle Wraps- 162
Late Night Nibblers- 211
Lobster Quesadillas- 55
Little Dawgies- 24
Little Shellys- 24
McGyver Breakfast- 76, 210
McMom Muffins- 211
Melon Molecules- 110
Mold Spore Burgers- 111
Mosquito Melons- 162
Movie Night Shoe Box- 210
Mud Potatoes- 75
Nacho Bar- 94
Nemo Nibblets- 55
Night Sky Sandwiches- 180
Osmosis Celery- 111
Octopus Sandwiches- 40, 56, 197
Panther Pockets- 162
Parrot Pinwheels- 163
Party Pizzas- 209
Peanut Butter & Jellyfish- 56
Petite Quiche- 149
Pigs in a Beach Towel- 131
Pigs in a Blanket- 23, 75, 215
Pigs in a Sleeping Bag- 78
Pinky Sandwiches- 148
Pirate Teeth- 195
Polly Pinwheels- 197
Popcorn Geyser- 110
Princess Pinwheels- 148
Puke Pizza- 41
Quick Berry Pancakes- 77
Radioactive Wraps- 111
Real Astronaut Food- 180

FOOD (con't)

Roasted Weenies- 75
Satellite Snacks- 180
Sausage Tot Casserole- 211
Savage Sausages- 162
Sea Snails- 56
Seaweed Pasta- 197
Seaworthy Sausage Stackers- 196
Scrambled Egg Pockets- 76
Sloppy Taco Bowls- 93
Soft Pretzel Lassos- 23
South of the Border Popcorn- 94
Spanish Rice- 95
Sticky Boogers- 40
Tortilla Shapes- 93
Trail Mix Party Starters- 73
Used Cotton Swab Snacks- 41
Veggie Pizza- 215
Veggies Cups- 74
Watermelon Ship- 196
What about Bob Kabobs- 76
Wild West Food- 22-24
Wormy Burgers- 40
Yogurt Parfaits- 148
Yogurt & Pudding Tubes- 179

DRINKS

Alien Punch- 182
Asteroid Soda- 182
Fantastic Island Punch- 133
Frankenstein Punch- 113
Fruit Smoothies- 166
Jungle Juice- 166
Lava Meets the Sea- 58
Lemonade Fizzies- 27
Magic Potion Punch- 152
Pink Lemonade Fizzies- 151
Pirate Ale- 199
Ruby Red Punch- 199
Sarsaparilla- 27
Seaweed Water- 58
Shark Punch- 58
Shirley Temples- 214
Slumber Party Punch- 214
Smoothies- 133
Spit Wad Sodas- 44
Toe Jam Punch- 44
Toxic Potion Drink- 113
Twinkie Shakes- 214
Watermelon Aqua Frescas- 97
Wicked Witch Cubes- 152
Wild West Drinks- 27

DESSERTS

Apple Enchiladas- 95
Apple Pie on a Stick- 77
Aquarium Cups- 57
Armpit Fudge- 42, 217
Biscuit Monkey Bread- 164
Brainy Cupcakes- 111
Brownie Pizza- 212
Brownie Smores- 25, 78
Cactus Cupcakes- 25
Cap 'n Crunch Treats- 198
Castle Cupcakes- 151
Cheetah Cake- 165
Cherry Chip Ice Cream Shortcakes- 150
Chicken Pox Pancakes- 42
Chocolate Sandwiches- 213
Chocolate Covered Strawberries- 150, 213
Cool Whip Cookies- 216
Crazy Crispy Treats- 112
Fairy Dust Crunch- 149
Fondue Dippables- 218
Frozen Soda Pop- 111
Fruity Pebble Cookies- 96
Fruity Pebble Treats- 132
Glow In the Dark Jell-O- 113, 181
Gorilla Popsicles- 164
Homemade Choros- 96
Horseshoe Biscuits- 25
Ice Cream Cone Smores- 212
Ice Cream Octopus- 57
Island Fondue- 132
Kitty Litter Cake- 43

Mad Science Ice Cream- 112
Magic Wand Pretzels- 149
Mars-Mallow Crispy Treats- 182
Mexican Flag Cupcake Cones- 96
Moon Landing Cake- 181
Moose Poop- 44
Mud Cups- 41
Muddy Snowball Cookies- 43
Octopops- 58
Oven Fried Fruit Pies- 26
Oven Pies- 216
PBJ Cookies- 218
Peanut Butter Zebra Poop- 165
Princess Surprise Cake- 151
Rainbow Swirl Cake- 214
Rattlesnake Cake- 26
Real Orange Sherbets- 132
Rice Crispy Treats- 214
Roasted Banana Boats- 78
Roasted Marshmallow- 77
Sand on My Cupcake- 132
Sandy Beach Cups- 57, 199
Seaweed- 56
Seven Seas Sunset Pops- 199
Strawberry Crunch- 213
Strawberry Roll Ups- 216
Strawberry Shortcake- 78
Sunken Treasure Cake- 198
Swamp Gunk- 42
Tiger Stripe Cookies- 164
Under the Sea Cake- 57
Unfried Ice Cream- 95
Volcano Cake- 131

ACTIVITIES

ABC Game- 80
Beachball Dodge Ball- 138
Bean and Spoon Relay- 99
Bottle Rockets- 186
Campfire Songs- 85-87
Cannonball Pop- 200
Card Games- 222-223
Cattle Drive- 28
Cheetah Chatter- 167
Clanking Cowbells- 32
Coconut Bowling- 139, 166
Coconut Cleanup- 135
Collecting Meteorites- 185
Cornstarch Capers- 45, 117
Crab Races- 61, 138
Crazy Fashion Show- 219
Ding Dong Spanish- 100
Dirty Diaper Sniff- 45
Dirty Lincolns- 118
Disappearing Act- 122
Donut Bobbing- 80
Donut Fisherman- 101
Dotted Nail Art- 220
Dry Ice- 124
Earth Defender- 185
Earthquake Ping Pong- 100
Edible Knots- 28
Erupting Volcano- 121
Facials and Pedicures- 221
Fairy Makeovers- 153
Fish Face Marathon- 61
Fish Stories- 59
Flashlight Limbo- 136
Flashlight Tag- 81

Floating Ice Cubes- 115
Floating Water- 116
Fruit Batteries- 118
Glowing Soda Comet- 186
Glowing Soda Geysers- 121
Going on a Safari- 167
Going on a Hike- 80
Guppy, Guppy, Shark- 59
Hanky Toss- 30
Heads up Hula Hoops- 135
Hole in My Bucket- 138
Horseshoes- 27, 31
Hot Potato- 28
How to Limbo- 136
Hula Marathon- 133
Human Knots Game- 168
Hunt the Dragon- 154
Hunting Seashells- 61
Instant Cottage Cheese- 116
Island Memory- 137
Jar of Lightning Bugs- 81
Jungle Suckers- 169
Karaoke- 220
Kiss the Frog- 154
Land Lubbers- 59
Learn to Hula Dance- 134
Lifesaver Lightning- 115
Magic Milk- 116
Magnet Mania- 117
Malia Races- 135
Man Eating Vines- 168
Marshmallow Wars- 47
Mexican Duck Pond- 99
Mexican Kickball- 102

ACTIVITIES (con't)

Mom Has Psychic Powers-114
Moon Rock Relay- 184
Mosquito Bites- 79, 168
Mummified Friends- 219
Musical Hats- 97
Musical Hippo Hop- 169
Musical Island Hop- 137
Musical Tiaras- 153
Obstacle Course- 79
Ocean Charades- 60
Open Real Coconuts- 134, 167
Pan For Gold- 30
Parrot Me- 200
Pass the Lasso- 28
Peanut Pushers- 169
Piñata- 98, 201
Ping Pong Hurricane- 98
Pirate Peg Leg Race- 202
Planet Twister- 183
Pok A Tot- 101
Popcorn-82
Popping Zits- 46
Princess' Purse- 153
Princess Secret Message- 153
Pudding Fling- 46
Puked On Piggies- 47
Rainbow Density Column- 119
Raising Raisins- 114
Rattlesnake Jump Rope- 101
Rattlesnake Rodeo- 31
Red Light Green Light- 82
Remote Control Rover- 183
Roping Broncos- 29
Royal Fashion Show- 152
Sack Races- 30

Safari Snapshots- 168
Saturn Ring Toss- 185
Scavenger Hunts- 81, 221, 233
Screaming Lincolns- 121
Seashell Hunter- 139
Secret Egg Trick- 115
Seed Spitting Contest- 31, 79
Seeking Lost Slipper- 152
Sharpshooter- 32
Ship Wars- 202
Silent Maracas- 98
Skunk Wars- 47
Sleeping Bag Races- 80
Sleeping Outside- 69
Slimy Spelling Bee- 44
Smartie Suckers- 154
Smells like Venus- 122
Smoke Bubbles- 121
Smoking Sugar Cubes- 114
Soda Geyser- 121
Space Blaster Battle- 186
Space Ship Runway- 186
Spaghetti Relay- 46
Straw Rocket Race- 184
Telescope- 187
The Captain Says- 68, 201
Tourist Tornado- 134
Treasure Dive- 201
Uh Um Err- 200
Walk the Plank- 200
Water Gun Showdown- 31
What in Tarnation- 29
Worm Hunt- 47
Worst Makeover Ever- 218

CRAFTS

African Drums- 169
Astronaut Glove Drawings- 188
Binoculars- 171
Captain Hooks- 203
CD Space Ships- 190
Clouds in a Bottle- 120
Coffee Can Clogs- 83
Cork Horses- 33
Design Your Flip Flops- 141
Dryer Lint Clay- 48
Easy Peasy Sand Art- 140
Fairy Butterflies- 156
Fairy Tissue Flowers- 156
Fake Poo- 49
Finger Weaving- 226
Fleece Fringe Pillows- 225
Friendship Pins- 224
Funky Flip Flops- 229
God's Eye- 83
Graffiti Shorts- 223
Hawaiian Sunglass Straps- 140
Hawaiian Tissue Flowers- 142
Hobby Horses- 34
Homemade Flubber- 48, 117
Homemade Glubber- 119
Homemade Kazoos- 84
Homemade Lava Lamp- 119
Homemade Orange Soda- 120
Homemade Rockets- 189
Homemade Silly Putty- 117
Inside Out Piñatas- 104
Instant Cacti- 33-34
Jars of Space- 188
Jars of Toxic Waste- 48
Jungle Masks- 170
Lasso Pencil Cups- 34
Leaf Rubbings- 84
Leather Bookmarks- 33
Make Your Own Galaxy- 189
Maracas- 103
Mexican Tissue Flowers- 102
Mexican Worry Dolls- 104
Moon Shoes- 188
No-sew Princess Skirts- 155
Ocean Globes- 61
Ojo De Dios- 102
Painted Fish- 64
Paper Plate Jellyfish- 63
Paper Quilling- 104
Parrot Buddy- 203
Pet Rocks- 84
Pie Plate Sun Catchers- 32, 103
Pinecone Birdfeeder- 83
Pirate Hats- 202
Princess Bracelets- 155
Princess Hats- 156
Rainsticks- 171
Ribbon Weave Barrettes- 228
Salt Dough Fun- 227
Salt Dough Sea Creatures- 64
Seashell Wind Chimes- 62, 139
Spyglass Telescope- 203
Stained Glass Tea Lights- 224
Stained Glass Wax Fish- 63
Sweet Castles- 155
Terra Cotta Crabs- 141
Tie Dye Socks- 225
Tissue Sea Animals- 62

USE THIS SPACE FOR YOUR OWN COOL PARTY IDEAS!

USE THIS SPACE TO PRACTICE WRITING A COOL REVIEW OF THIS BOOK!

Made in the USA
Lexington, KY
17 September 2011